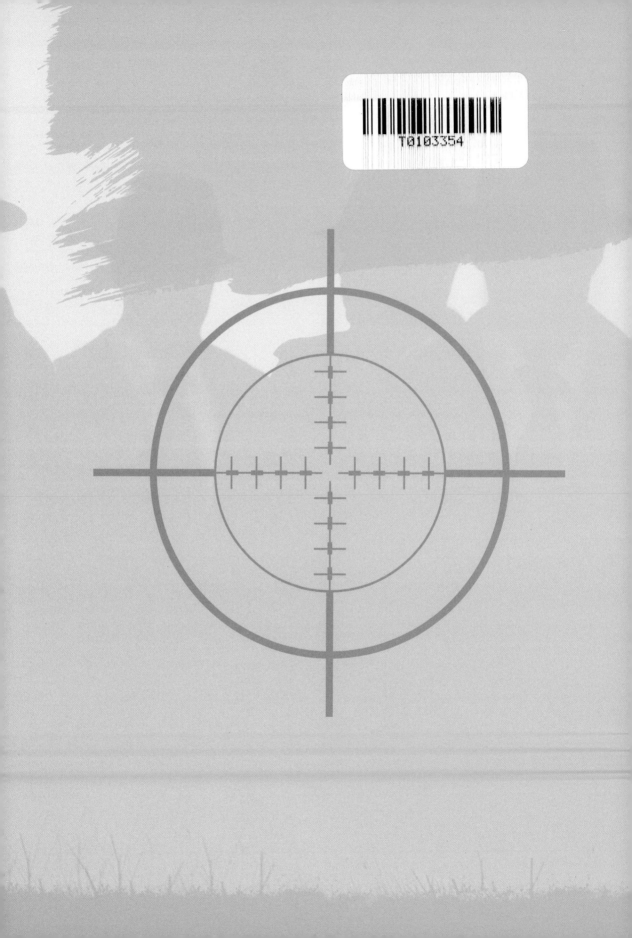

CONSPIRACIES

CONSPIRACIES
HISTORY'S GREATEST PLOTS, COLLUSIONS AND COVER UPS

CHARLOTTE GREIG
AND MIKE ROTHSCHILD

SIRIUS

SIRIUS

This edition published in 2024 by Sirius Publishing, a division of
Arcturus Publishing Limited,
26/27 Bickels Yard, 151–153 Bermondsey Street,
London SE1 3HA

ISBN: 978-1-3988-3728-7
AD011017UK

Printed in China

CONTENTS

INTRODUCTION 6

CHAPTER 1
THEY'VE GOT YOUR NUMBER 13
EDWARD SNOWDEN:
   BIG BROTHER IS WATCHING YOU 15
FLIGHT MH370:
   THE GREAT DISAPPEARING ACT 18
GARETH WILLIAMS: THE BODY IN THE BAG 22
ALEXANDER LITVINENKO:
   DEATH OF A DOUBLE AGENT 26
HAARP AND ELF WAVES 30
RFID CHIPS 34
CHEMTRAILS 38

CHAPTER 2
MURDER MYSTERIES 42
WHO SHOT JFK? 44
THE ASSASSINATION OF MALCOLM X 50
THE DEATH OF DIANA, PRINCESS OF WALES 54
JOHN LENNON AND THE FBI 59
THE CLINTON BODY COUNT 62

CHAPTER 3
SECRET SOCIETIES 67
THE BILDERBERG GROUP 69
THE ILLUMINATI 73
GOD'S BANKER:
   THE DEATH OF ROBERTO CALVI 78
SECRETS OF THE CATHOLIC CHURCH 82
THE PROTOCOLS OF THE ELDERS OF ZION 86
THE GEMSTONE FILES 90
THE REPTILE ELITE 94
THE ROTHSCHILD BANKING FAMILY 98
THE NEW WORLD ORDER 104

CHAPTER 4
POLITICAL CONSPIRACIES 109
WATERGATE 110
THE IRAN-CONTRA CONSPIRACY 116
THE CIA AND SALVADOR ALLENDE 120
CHAPPAQUIDDICK 124
FALSE FLAG SHOOTINGS 128
AGENDA 21 AND THE UN 134

CHAPTER 5
MYSTERIES AND THE UNKNOWN 139
FLYING SAUCERS: THE ROSWELL INCIDENT 140
THE RENDLESHAM AFFAIR 146
CROP CIRCLES 150
THE MEN IN BLACK 154
THE MOON LANDINGS 158
AREA 51 AND UFO DISCLOSURE 162
NIBIRU/PLANET X 166

CHAPTER 6
COVER-UPS 171
THE WACO INCIDENT 172
THE CRASH OF TWA FLIGHT 800 178
MIND CONTROL: MKULTRA 182
THE TUSKEGEE SYPHILIS EXPERIMENT 186
THE CIA AND AIDS 190
FLAT EARTH 194
THE MONTAUK PROJECT 198
CERN 202

INDEX 206
PICTURE CREDITS 208

INTRODUCTION

Often enough, yesterday's conspiracy theory is today's accepted history. If you'd said at the time that Hitler started the Reichstag Fire himself to smear his Communist opposition you'd have been called paranoid. Now it's an accepted fact. And how many people today really believe that JFK was assassinated by Lee Harvey Oswald acting all alone? And are we wrong to see conspiracies in the links between, say, the US government and Halliburton or Enron? Or naïve not to?

Of course, not all conspiracy theories have a basis in fact. Some are outlandish, such as the theory that the world is hollow and inhabited at the centre; others, such as the notion that the government is hushing up alien visitations here, there and everywhere, seem like the stuff of *X-Files* episodes. Yet all of them, even the most bizarre, address facts that cannot easily be explained, or point to our psychological need to find a reason for everything that takes place in our world.

Then there are those conspiracy theories that hover entertainingly on the edge of possibility: for example, the idea that the moon landings were faked up in a film studio. And, of course, there's not a celebrity death without its attendant conspiracy theory. Was Princess Diana murdered? Was the FBI really behind John Lennon's murder? To some, these theories simply demonstrate our human tendency to deny death and loss, to let our idols go; to others, they reveal the sinister currents of money and power that run below the public life of any celebrated figure in our culture today.

This book gathers together some of the most compelling conspiracies in the modern world: ranging from the genuinely credible to the frankly implausible, from mind control conspiracies to crop circles, from the death of Alexander Litvinenko to the Holy Grail. Was Pearl Harbor a set-up? Does our society contain a reptilian elite? We may not have the answers, but we've got some pretty good theories!

WHAT IS A CONSPIRACY THEORY?

The word 'conspiracy' comes from the Latin *conspirare*. Literally it means 'to breathe together'. In practice, it refers to two or more people making a plan of action that other parties are not told about. Theoretically that plan could be either good or bad, but over the centuries it has gained a distinctly negative sense. You can see this clearly from the way in which the word is used in the legal sphere: 'conspiracy' in a legal sense always refers to wrongdoing.

Conspiracies are not by definition secret, but as the word has attached itself to criminal behaviour that's almost inevitably a part of the package. So, over the years, secrecy has become a part of our conventional sense of what a conspiracy is. And it's a crucial part when it comes to the development of conspiracy theories. Essentially, conspiracy theories are alternative explanations of history or of the world about us. Conspiracy theories suggest that dramatic events happen not by accident or for apparent reasons, but because of plans made in secrecy.

There's no doubt that conspiracy theories have been with us for thousands of years. After all, conspiracies certainly have. Whether it's the ancient Greeks conspiring to take over Troy or the Caesar's rivals

At the time of the Reichstag Fire in February 1933, the idea that Hitler might have started it himself seemed like an outlandish conspiracy theory – today it is widely accepted as fact.

conspiring to assassinate him, history is full of dramatic conspiracies. And there have always been people with a suspicious cast of mind who've come up with conspiracy theories to explain such events.

However, it's only in the past hundred years or so that conspiracy theories have really come to the fore. Perhaps that has something to do with the decline of religion. In the past people tended to see inexplicable events as the work of the Almighty. In our more secular times, however, people tend to look for the nefarious hand of man.

The late nineteenth century saw the birth of some enduring conspiracy theories. As the world was changing fast through industrialization, and the old certainties of life were being shattered, many people started to suspect that there was some powerful organization controlling all this, some group who were effectively setting themselves up as rivals to God. The prime candidates for this role, in a Europe in which anti-Semitism had long been rife, were the Jewish communities. The idea of an international Jewish conspiracy began to gain credence, especially in Russia in the turbulent years leading up to World War I. Other candidates for the role of secret rulers of the world included the Freemasons, the Communists, and the semi-mythical group known as the Illuminati.

Such visions of a world controlled by a small and sinister cabal are still a popular element in conspiracy theories today. In fact, they lie behind almost every conspiracy theory there is. So perhaps the answer to the question 'what is a conspiracy theory?' should be 'it's a theory which suggests that the great world events are not what they seem; rather, they are the manifestations of a world controlled by a secret elite.'

CONSPIRACY THEORIES TODAY

There has been an explosion of interest in conspiracy theories in recent years. There are many possible reasons for this – loss of faith in religion, as mentioned previously, loss of faith in politicians, a sensationalist mass media that likes to broadcast sensational theories, the influence of films and novels espousing conspiracies, and so on. One major factor is undoubtedly the growth of the internet. The internet is the perfect medium for spreading conspiracy theories. Where once a rumour would be passed around a chosen few insiders and spread slowly through the metropolitan grapevine – for example the one about the identity of the Watergate source known as 'Deep Throat' – these days, it will be on the internet in minutes and instantly transmitted around the world.

Thus today, when a major event occurs, conspiracy

theories immediately start to circulate on the internet. Evidence that the authorities would prefer to have kept quiet is now available to be discussed and interpreted from America to Australia. The trouble is, of course, that so too are lies, fabrications, and delusions. The internet is at once a marvellous tool for avoiding censorship and allowing the voice of truth to emerge, and also a forum in which every lunatic and partisan commentator can have their say in the era of 'fake news'. Today, when so many conspiracy theories appear on the internet, it is sometimes a difficult business to determine which ones are worthy of serious consideration and which are simply hearsay.

The internet provides the perfect vehicle for conspiracy theories to spread.

POLITICAL CONSPIRACIES

This book will attempt to offer an unbiased investigation into several aspects of state surveillance in the digital age and leave the reader to make up their own mind. We'll try to make sense of the mysterious last moments of Flight MH370, the plane that disappeared. We'll also look into some of the classic political mysteries of yesteryear, such as the Watergate and Chappaquiddick conspiracies.

Coming closer to the present, we'll examine the string of suspicious deaths and assassinations that occurred during the 1960s. The most celebrated of these, the murder of JFK, is perhaps the ultimate conspiracy theory, with endless books, films and TV programmes devoted to it. The murder of radical black American leader Malcolm X has also attracted its fair share of speculation, and we'll also discuss this.

Many conspiracy theories relate to the existence of Secret Societies, and we'll be looking into several of these. We'll investigate The Bilderberg Group and attempt to establish whether this shadowy group is really running our world. And who, or what, is the Illuminati? Formed in 1776, have its members, 'the illuminated ones,' really been the secret power behind the throne throughout modern history?

Religion has always attracted its share of conspiracy theories, too, so we'll take a tour around the strange stories that surround the Holy Grail. Could Mary Magdalen have smuggled Christianity's most precious relic out of the Holy Land and into Western Europe, where it remains hidden to this day? Closer to the present, there is the bizarre death of Roberto Calvi, nicknamed 'God's banker'. Could the Pope's business chiefs really have been hand in glove with the Mafia?

STRANGER THAN FICTION

And here we move onto the theories that read like the stuff of science fiction. One of the most enduring conspiracy theories of this type maintains that the moon landings were faked. Could this possibly be true? And what of extraterrestrial happenings and alien visitation? What really happened at Roswell? Or at Rendlesham Forest? And how can we explain crop circles?

Conspiracy theories, then, come in all shapes and sizes. There are those that seem to be taken from the pages of science fiction novels or thrillers. Indeed, many of them do crop up in popular fiction, not least Dan Brown's enormously popular *Da Vinci Code*, which draws from a whole tradition of Holy Grail conspiracies dating back for over a thousand years. Yet while many conspiracy theories are more entertaining than realistic, there are some that reveal genuinely disturbing information and ask important questions about secrecy in the way we are governed and receive information.

In the end it is for you, the reader, to decide which theories to believe, and which to dismiss. So prepare to enter into a world much stranger than fiction: the world of the conspiracy theory.

A wealth of conspiracy theories surrounds the Holy Grail.

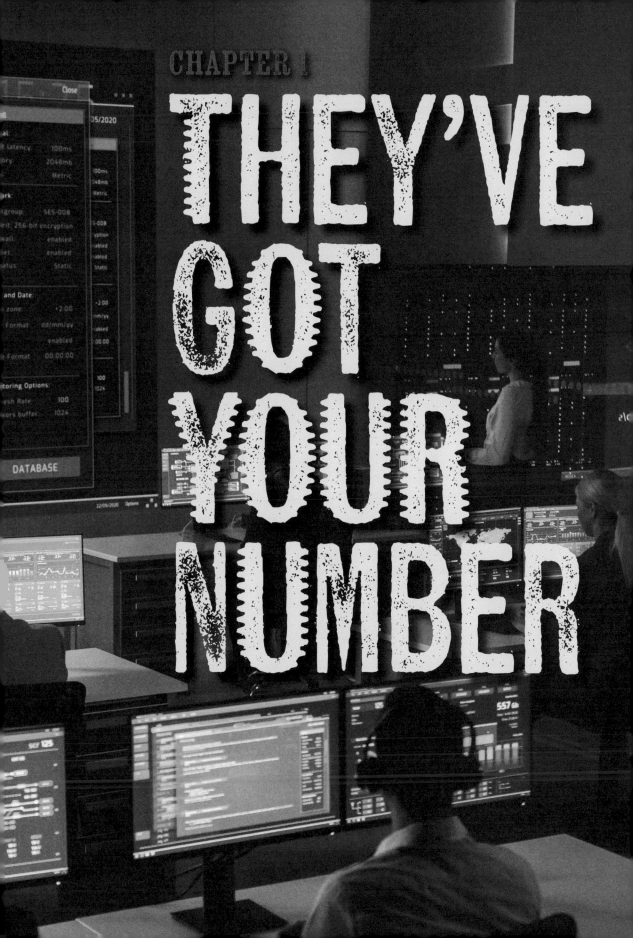

CHAPTER 1

THEY'VE GOT YOUR NUMBER

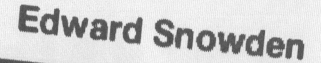

Edward Snowden

Edward Snowden, former CIA agent turned whistleblower, accepted asylum in Russia.

Snowden during interview with Glenn Greenv and Laura Poitras (June 6, 2013).

Born   Edward Joseph Snowden
June 21, 1983 (age 31)
Elizabeth City, North Carolina,
United States of America

and

EDWARD SNOWDEN: BIG BROTHER IS WATCHING YOU

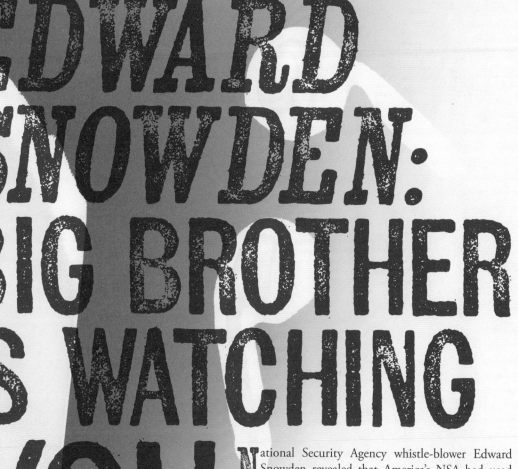

National Security Agency whistle-blower Edward Snowden revealed that America's NSA had used a top-secret 'black budget' to spy on some of the US's closest allies, including France, Germany, Spain, Mexico, Brazil, China and even Britain, whose Government Communications Headquarters (GCHQ) operated in collaboration with the NSA under the Five Eyes agreement, along with Canada, Australia and New Zealand. It also tapped the phones of 122 world leaders, including Angela Merkel's. Indeed, the NSA and GCHQ operated a worldwide conspiracy monitoring the phone calls, texts and emails of countless individuals, companies and institutions, including those of its own citizens.

Snowden joined the CIA in 2006 as a computer systems administrator at the global communications division in the agency's headquarters at Langley, Virginia. After ten months, he was posted to Geneva where he learned the tricks of the intelligence trade, such as getting 'targets' drunk enough to end up in jail, then bailing them out so that they would be in your debt and become informants.

In 2009, he quit the CIA and joined Dell, a major contractor to the NSA. Posted to the NSA offices at Yokota air base outside Tokyo, he taught officials and military officers how to defend their networks from hackers. There he was exposed to live NSA monitors showing targeted killings in the Middle East, watching as military and CIA drones turned people into body parts. He also learned about the NSA's mass surveillance capabilities and their ability to map the movement of everyone in a city by monitoring their MAC addresses, a unique identifier emitted by each mobile phone, computer and electronic device.

STATE SNOOPING

Three years later, he was posted to the CIA's information-sharing office in Hawaii. This was supposed to be monitoring activities in China and North Korea. Instead it was global exchange and he was horrified to discover that the content of communications – as well as the metadata – from millions of emails and phone calls made by Palestinian- and Arab-Americans was being handed over to the Israelis. No attempt was made to disguise their identities even though they might have had relatives living in the occupied territories who could become targets on the basis of these intercepts.

The NSA also spied on the pornography-viewing habits of political radicals in case it could be used against them. Snowden said he complained to his superiors about these illegal activities. When nothing was done, he began to download files which he would later leak to the media. He then moved on to the NSA's Threat Operations Center at Fort Meade, Maryland,

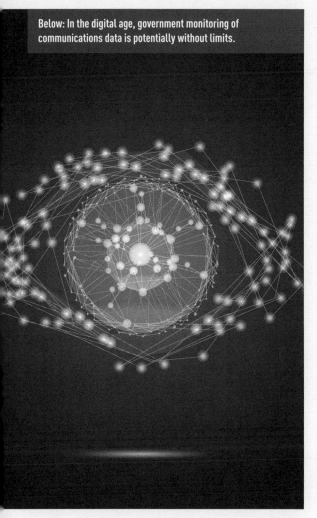

where he collected more evidence of the agency's illegal surveillance.

TRAITOR OR PATRIOT?

Snowden said that the moment he decided to blow the whistle was when he saw the Director of National Intelligence James Clapper lie under oath to Congress. On 12 March 2013, Clapper was testifying to the Senate Select Committee on Intelligence, when Senator Ron Wyden asked him: 'Does the NSA collect any type of data at all on millions, or hundreds of millions, of Americans?'

Clapper responded: 'No, sir…. Not wittingly. There are cases where they could inadvertently, perhaps, collect, but not wittingly.'

Snowden knew this was untrue. The NSA logged nearly every telephone call Americans make. It also bugged European Union offices in Washington and Brussels and, with GCHQ, has tapped the Continent's major fibre-optic communications cables. Thirty-eight embassies and missions were on its list of surveillance targets, including those belonging to allies such as France, Japan and Mexico.

As an 'infrastructure analyst', Snowden's job was to look for new ways to break into internet and telephone traffic around the world. This gave him access to lists of devices all over the world that the NSA had hacked. He also discovered that, as well as hoovering up staggering amounts of information, the NSA had developed cyberweapons so it could, if necessary, go on the attack. The NSA and Israel co-wrote the Stuxnet computer worm used to sabotage Iran's nuclear programme.

ON THE RUN

In May 2013, Snowden fled with four laptop computers thought to contain the files he had downloaded. There he began briefing journalists. On 6 June, the *Guardian* printed a story saying that the NSA had been given permission to collect the telephone records of the millions of customers of the US telecoms giant Verizon. The order had been granted by the secret Foreign Intelligence Surveillance Court. The following day the *Guardian* and the *Washington Post* reported the NSA was accessing the systems of US internet giants including Google and Facebook, and collecting data under a clandestine surveillance programme called Prism. Since 2007, this programme had allowed the NSA to collect material including emails, live chats and search histories. GCHQ also had access to Prism.

Then the *Guardian* revealed the existence of another program called Boundless Informant that gave analysts summaries of the NSA's worldwide data collection activities by counting metadata. It showed that the NSA was collecting more information on Americans in the United States than on Russians in Russia despite repeated assurances to Congress that it could not keep track of all the surveillance it performs on American communications.

In the US, Snowden was branded a traitor and he was charged with espionage and theft. Offered asylum in Ecuador, he found his US passport revoked, leaving him stranded at Moscow's Sheremetyevo International Airport while changing planes there. After 39 days in the transit lounge, Snowden accepted asylum in Russia. Despite attempts to shut him up, evidence of a global conspiracy to spy on friend and foe alike, on an unprecedented scale, conducted by the NSA and GCHQ continued to come out.

FLIGHT MH370 DISAPPEARING

The disappearance of Flight MH370 remains one of the greatest mysteries in aviation history. How was it possible to evade the tracking systems of so many different authorities?

n 8 March 2014, Malaysian Airlines Flight MH370 took off from Kuala Lumpur International Airport bound for Beijing with 239 people on board. Less than an hour into the flight, radio contact was lost and the plane vanished from air traffic controllers' radar screens. Only later was it discovered that Malaysian military radar had continued to track the plane as it veered westwards across the Malay Peninsula, then northwest up the Straits of Malacca towards the Andaman Sea.

Eventually, sophisticated analysis of the satellite communication from the plane's automated systems indicated that it had then turned southwards and the search moved to the South Indian Ocean. One piece of debris, a flaperon broken off from the wing, washed up on the French island of Réunion, some 2,500 miles west of the search area, on 29 July 2015. Since then, other small pieces of wreckage that might have come from the wings and engine of the missing aircraft have been found along the coast of east Africa where oceanographers said that currents would have carried debris from the search area. However, a search of the sea floor where the plane was supposed to have crashed, lasting three years and costing $130 million (£105m), could find no sign of the huge fuselage of the Boeing 777. And if the plane had broken up on impact how come none of the debris you would expect to float – seat cushions, life jackets, luggage, even corpses – had ended up floating in the sea?

THE GREAT ACT

STRANGE EVENTS

This has spawned all sorts of conspiracy theories – from a hijacking gone wrong to pilot suicide, an accidental shoot-down alien abduction, and even that it had been substituted for MH17, shot down over Ukraine three months later. One of the most intriguing came from aviation expert Jeff Wise, who led CNN's coverage of the disappearance of MH370. It centred on the fact that 20 employees of Freescale Semiconductors, an avionics firm said to specialize in stealth technology, were on board.

Wise noted that the plane was initially assumed to have flown north from the Andaman Sea and Malaysian prime minister Najib Razak had appealed to the president of Kazakhstan, Nursultan Nazarbayev, formerly first secretary of the Communist Party of Kazakhstan and an ally of Vladimir Putin, to allow Malaysia to set up a search in Kazakhstan. Only later was it thought that the plane had travelled south to crash into the sea in one of the remotest spots on Earth.

Re-examining the satellite data, Wise and the Independent Group, a band of like-minded aviation experts, decided that the plane had indeed flown north while bogus data had been fed to the satellite.

Checking the passenger list, he found that two Ukrainians and a Russian were on board. Little was known about them except that the Ukrainians came from Odessa, a former Soviet naval base, and the

Russian's hobby was scuba-diving. He was sitting up front in business class, with the two Ukrainians further back in economy.

Wise reckons that the Russian came on to the plane with a bag of scuba gear, containing three full-face diving masks. Once the plane had reached cruising altitude and the cabin staff were looking the other way, he slipped into the electronics-and-equipment – or E/E – bay, which, on the Boeing 777, could be accessed through a hatch at the front of the first-class cabin. From there, he could control all the systems on the plane.

First he would have cut off all communication, then plugged in portable equipment that would upload false satellite data to the system. From the E/E bay, he could depressurize the cabin while he and his two accomplices breathed oxygen through their diving masks.

INSIDE JOB

As he turned the plane to the west, the flight crew would have spotted that something was wrong. But there would have been nothing they could do about it. None of their checklists would have covered a possible hijacking from the E/E bay. The anti-hijacking lock on the cockpit door could also be controlled from there. When it was opened, two burly men wearing oxygen masks entered, giving the hijackers total control of the plane.

While the crew and passengers lapsed into unconsciousness, the plane flew across the Malay Peninsula along the Malaysian–Thai border, where it was unlikely that anyone would be looking out for a rogue aircraft. Then the plane turned again and flew up the Straits of Malacca between Thailand and Indonesia.

Instead of turning southwards, Wise reckons that

Australian ships search for evidence of the debris from MH370 in April 2014.

Flight MH370 continued northwards to Kazakhstan, sending its last electronic 'handshake' to the satellite near the Baikonur Cosmodrome in Kazakhstan, which is leased by Russia to launch the rockets supplying the space station. Baikonur had a runway nearly 15,000 ft (4.6 km/2.8 miles) long, built to land the Buran space plane, the Soviet Union's version of the Space Shuttle, whose programme was cancelled in 1993. This is the only airstrip in the world built specifically for self-landing aeroplanes and the 777 has an auto-landing system. That meant that even someone who had no experience flying commercial aircraft could land the plane safely.

THE PLANE TRUTH?

However, Baikonur is in the middle of a flat, treeless plain, a difficult place to hide something as big as a Boeing 777, and the hijackers would have had just 90 minutes to hide it before the sun came up. Studying satellite imagery, Wise noted that a huge building at Baikonur, which had been left to rot after the Buran project had been abandoned, had recently been demolished. Where it had been, there was now a large patch, around the size of a 777, covered with rubble where the plane could be hidden.

Wise says he can offer no motive for the hijacking. However, both during the Vietnam War and World War II, the Soviets seized American and Allied prisoners who had specialized technical knowledge. If the cabin had been repressurized after the hijackers had taken over the plane, the 20 employees of Freescale could now be producing the latest stealth cloaking systems for the Russians.

The sun rises over the launch pad at the Baikonur Cosmodrome in Kazakhstan. Could this be the final resting place of Flight MH370?

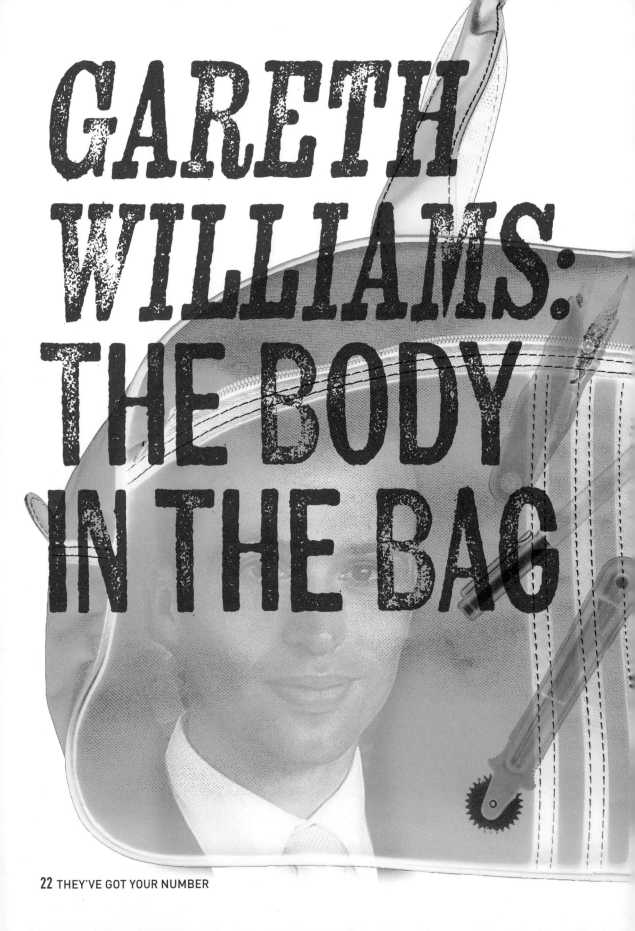

GARETH WILLIAMS: THE BODY IN THE BAG

On Monday, 23 August 2010, GCHQ code-breaker Gareth Williams failed to turn up for work again at the Secret Intelligence Service, commonly known as MI6, where he had been seconded. No one had seen him for over a week.

The police were sent round to the Security Service flat in Pimlico, London – not far from the world-famous Tate Britain art gallery – where he was staying. After forcing entry, officers found his body – naked and decomposing – inside a red sports holdall. It had been padlocked from the outside, but the key was inside the bag, under Williams' body. There were no injuries on the body and no indications that he had struggled against an attacker, or tried to escape.

WRAPPED IN AN ENIGMA

The bag was in the bath, but no finger-, foot- or palm-prints or DNA belonging to Williams were found on the rim of the bath, or on the padlock or zipper, and he was not wearing any gloves. There was no sign of a break-in and the heating in the flat had been turned up, even though it was mid-summer, which helped speed up decomposition. Toxicology examinations showed no trace of alcohol or drugs and an initial post-mortem proved inconclusive. Nothing was missing from the flat and a couple seen leaving the building were soon ruled out of the investigation.

Williams' family believe that his death was linked to his work at SIS and that fingerprints, DNA and other evidence had been wiped from the scene as part of a deliberate cover-up. Indeed, the authorities were plainly sensitive about the

A red sports holdall of the type in which Gareth Williams' body was found.

investigation. Foreign Secretary at the time William Hague signed a public immunity certificate authorizing the withholding of the details of Williams' secret work and exempting officers of America's National Security Agency and the FBI that Williams had worked with from testifying at the inquest. SIS chief Sir John Sawers also met with the commissioner of the Metropolitan Police Sir Paul Stephenson to discuss how the investigation would be handled and who would head it.

THE MYSTERY DEEPENS

As a direct result the coroner, Dr Fiona Wilcox, was critical of the police's handling of the investigation. Officers in the Met's counter-terrorism branch, SO15, whose role was to interview SIS witnesses, failed to take formal statements and withheld information from the senior investigating officer, Detective Chief Inspector Jackie Sebire.

The coroner also criticized the handling of an iPhone belonging to Williams and found in his work locker, which contained deleted images of him naked in a pair of boots. An iPhone found in his living room had recently been wiped and restored to factory settings. LGC Forensics were also criticized over DNA contamination, and the coroner's office was censured for failing to inform police officers of a second post-mortem.

Wilcox dismissed evidence of Williams' interest in bondage and cross-dressing as irrelevant. Only a tiny percentage of his internet browsing involved visiting bondage sites. Williams was naked in the bag, not dressed in women's clothing, and she condemned leaks to the media about him cross-dressing as a possible attempt 'by some third party to manipulate a section of the evidence'.

The idea that he had locked himself in the bag for some auto-erotic thrill was also ruled out. The coroner said that Williams was a 'scrupulous risk assessor' – if he had locked himself into the bag, he would have taken a knife in with him to aid his escape.

Her conclusion was that Williams was probably alive when put in the bag but probably suffocated very soon afterwards either from CO_2 poisoning, hypercapnia, or the effects of a short-acting poison. Passing a narrative verdict (one which does not attribute a cause to a named individual), she said she was satisfied that 'a third party placed the bag in the bath and on the balance of probabilities locked the bag'. Therefore, again on the balance of probabilities, he had been killed unlawfully.

Scotland Yard spent another year investigating the case, only to re-affirm its original conclusions – that Williams was alone at the time of his death, had locked himself inside the bag and died when he could not get out again. This directly contradicted the coroner's findings and was thought extremely unlikely by experts.

FRESH CLAIMS

Allegations then surfaced that Williams had been working with the NSA tracking money siphoned out of Moscow by the Russian Mafia. Cars registered to the Russian Embassy were spotted near his Pimlico flat in the days before his body was discovered. There were indications that someone had broken in through a skylight the day after the body had been found and tampered with the evidence.

Then KGB defector Boris Karpichkov, exiled in the UK, said that Williams had discovered a Russian agent inside GCHQ after a bungled attempt to recruit him as a double agent by blackmailing him over his private life. Consequently, he had to be killed. This was done by short-lived poison injected in his ear. The heating was turned up in the flat so that traces of the toxin would break down before the body was found.

There was also speculation that the SIS might have been responsible. Fearing that Williams might be a whistle-blower, they had bumped him off. With their close co-operation with the police, this would be easy to cover up.

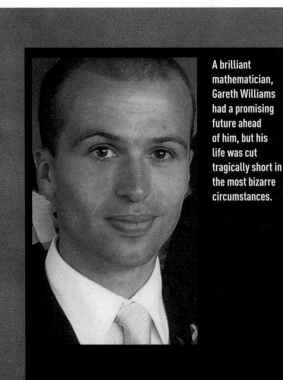

A brilliant mathematician, Gareth Williams had a promising future ahead of him, but his life was cut tragically short in the most bizarre circumstances.

Boris Karpichkov, a Russian double agent who defected to Britain, said that Williams had uncovered information that meant he had to be killed.

ALEXANDER
DEATH OF A

Alexander Litvinenko was a high flier in the KGB. He excelled in the Federal Security Service, or FSB, which replaced the KGB after the collapse of the Soviet Union. Through his work in counter-intelligence he met oligarch Boris Berezovsky. This did not endear him to his boss at the FSB Vladmir Putin and Litvinenko claimed he was given orders to assassinate Berezovsky. Going public, he appeared at a press conference revealing the conspiracy to kill Berezovsky and fellow dissident intelligence officer Mikhail Trepashkin. As a result, Litvinenko was dismissed from the FSB. Putin said: 'I fired Litvinenko and disbanded his unit… because FSB officers should not stage press conferences. This is not their job. And they should not make internal scandals public.'

Evading arrest, Litvinenko and his family fled to Turkey where he applied for asylum at the US Embassy. When this was denied, he flew to the UK where he was granted asylum in 2001. Five years later, he naturalized as a British citizen.

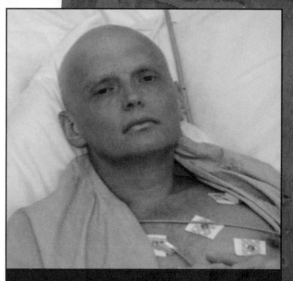

Litvinenko released a picture from his deathbed, blaming his former boss at the FSB Vladimir Putin for his demise.

LITVINENKO: DOUBLE AGENT

SPY IN EXILE

In Britain, he joined Boris Berezovsky, who had also fled to the UK, in his campaign against Putin. He also worked for MI6, though in the tradition of the service they will not confirm this. In his book *Blowing Up Russia*, Litvinenko claimed the Russian security services were complicit in a series of apartment block bombings in 1999 that killed more than 300 people, part of a coup to bring Putin to power. He also asserted that FSB agents trained al-Qaeda leaders in Dagestan and were involved in the 9/11 attacks. In 2002, he was convicted *in absentia* in Russia and sentenced to three and a half years for corruption, and Trepashkin, then in jail, warned him that an FSB unit had been assigned to assassinate him.

In a series of newspaper articles, Litvinenko claimed that the FSB were complicit in the 2002 Moscow theatre siege, the 2004 Beslan school massacre and numerous other terrorist attacks. According to Litvinenko, former prime minister of Italy and president of the European

Commission Romano Prodi had also worked for the KGB. However, perhaps his most damaging allegation was that Vladimir Putin, by then president of the Russian Federation, had ordered the assassination of dissident journalist Anna Politkovskaya. There were wilder accusations – that Putin was involved in drug running, even that he was a paedophile.

FATEFUL MEETING

On 1 November 2006, Litvinenko met two former KGB officers, Andrei Lugovoy and Dmitry Kovtun, in the Pine Bar of the Millennium Hotel in Mayfair. Then he had lunch with Italian nuclear-waste expert Mario Scaramella at Itsu, a sushi restaurant in Piccadilly. Afterwards he fell ill. Suffering from diarrhoea and vomiting, he found he could not walk and was taken to hospital. His throat was blistered; he could barely swallow, let alone talk. But he managed to register under the name of 'Edwin Carter' and medical staff at first laughed off the suspicions he voiced until they referred the case to Scotland Yard after Litvinenko had told them who he really was. It was thought he had been poisoned with thallium. His hair fell out and a picture of him on his deathbed was released. 'I want the world to see what they did to me,' Litvinenko said. In a final statement, he blamed Vladimir Putin for his death.

On 22 November, Alexander Litvinenko died of heart failure. His body was later found to contain more than 200 times the lethal dose of the radioactive element polonium. Detectives from Scotland Yard found they could trace three trails of radioactive polonium – belonging respectively to Litvinenko, Lugovoy and Kovtun. Passengers on board the planes Lugovoy and Kovtun had flown back to Moscow with were warned to contact the Department of Health. Meanwhile, the UK Atomic Weapons Establishment traced the source of the polonium to the Ozersk nuclear power plant, near the city of Chelyabinsk in Russia.

JUSTICE DENIED

The British government requested the extradition of Lugovoy to face charges relating to Litvinenko's death. The request was denied. Kovtun was under investigation by the German authorities for suspected plutonium smuggling, but Germany dropped the case in 2009.

There can be little doubt why Litvinenko was killed. Two days after he died, representative Sergei Abeltsev told the Russian Duma: 'The deserved punishment reached the traitor. I am confident that this terrible death will be a serious warning to traitors of all colours, wherever they are located. In Russia, they do not pardon treachery. I would recommend citizen Berezovsky to avoid any food at the commemoration for his accomplice Litvinenko.'

After US security analyst Paul Joyal alleged that Litvinenko had been killed as a warning to all critics of the Putin government, he was shot outside his home in Maryland. Surviving several assassination attempts, Boris Berezovsky was then found dead in suspicious circumstances in his house at Sunninghill near Ascot in Berkshire on 23 March 2013. The verdict? Suicide.

As regards Litvinenko, Dmitry Kovtun and Andrei Lugovoy denied any wrongdoing, but a leaked US diplomatic cable revealed that Kovtun had left traces of polonium in the house and car he had used in Hamburg.

TEA AND TREACHERY

Noberto Andrade, head barman of the Pine Bar at the Millennium Hotel, served tea and gin-and-tonics to Litvinenko and his companions on 1 November 2006. He claimed a distraction was created while he was serving the drinks. Polonium was found on the picture above where Litvinenko was sitting and on the table, chair and floor, leading detectives to believe that the poison had been delivered by aerosol spray.

After the three men left the bar, Andrade cleared the table and noticed the contents of the teapot had turned a funny colour.

'When I poured the remains of the teapot into the sink, the tea looked more yellow than usual and was thicker – it looked gooey,' he said. 'I scooped it out of the sink and threw it into the bin. I was so lucky I didn't put my fingers into my mouth, or scratch my eye as I could have got this poison inside me.'

The dishwasher, the bar and the sink were all found to have been contaminated. For weeks Andrade ran a temperature and suffered a throat infection. He feared for the safety of his wife and family, and doctors told him he faced an increased risk of contracting cancer in later life.

The Millennium Hotel, where staff working in the Pine Bar tested positive for polonium-210, the isotope that killed Litvinenko.

SALISBURY POISONING

In a case remarkably similar to that of Litvinenko, former Russian military intelligence officer and British spy Sergei Skripal and his daughter Yulia Skripal were poisoned in Salisbury, England, with a Novichok nerve agent on 4 March 2018. Developed in Russia, Novichok is thought to be one of the deadliest nerve agents ever produced.

Sergei Skripal was an officer for Russia's Main Intelligence Directorate, the GRU, and worked as a double agent for Britain's Secret Intelligence Service from 1995 until his arrest in Moscow in December 2004. Convicted of high treason, he was sentenced to thirteen years in a penal colony in 2006. He was released and settled in England in 2010 after a spy swap. Yulia remained in Russia and was visiting her father. One theory was that the Russian secret services had somehow tricked her into carrying the deadly poison.

Britain maintained that the poisoning had been carried out by the Russian secret services and that was likely to have been ordered by Vladimir Putin himself. Sixty Russian diplomats were expelled from Britain. The Russians responded in kind. More than twenty other countries expelled Russian diplomats in support of the UK. Russia claimed that it had nothing to do with the poisoning and that Britain had the means and the motive to murder Skripal.

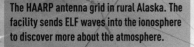

Located in rural Alaska is a government-created transmitter array that conspiracy theorists believe has the power to harness Extremely Low Frequency (ELF) waves to manipulate the weather, alter the electromagnetic makeup of the atmosphere and even to control minds and cause pain. Its name: HAARP, or High Frequency Active Auroral Research Program.

Since its construction in 1993 by the US Air Force, HAARP has been used to study plasma physics, electron emissions, how atmospheric disturbances affect GPS signals and to observe meteors and solar flares. Because it takes an enormous amount of power to generate ELF waves, HAARP uses a bit of a shortcut, turning the ionosphere into a giant ELF transmitter by hitting it with focused high frequency radio waves. Those waves can then be directed towards either land, the upper atmosphere or the ocean, depending on the subject of the experiment being carried out. In particular, HAARP

HAARP AND ELF WAVES

studies have helped determine how the ionosphere affects communication between submarines and satellites, as ELF waves move more easily through water than air.

But to conspiracy theorists, HAARP is nothing less than a machine that imbues the powers that be with a mind-boggling array of ways to control us and punish those who step out of line. And it's not just conspiracy cranks who think this way. A number of prominent researchers have expressed reservations about HAARP's

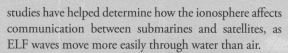

The governor of Minnesota from 1999 to 2003, Jesse Ventura, was concerned that the site was being used by the government for mind control or weather manipulation. His request to visit the facility was denied.

Conspiracy theorists believe that the work at HAARP is a development of the research done by Nikola Tesla toward the end of his life.

work is complex, esoteric and done in a remote part of the country. Hence, the conspiracy theories trying to figure out what it 'really' does.

ANGELS DON'T PLAY THIS HAARP

power, including the brother of a former US Senator, several renowned physicists and military officers and former Minnesota governor Jesse Ventura. ELF waves have been blamed for the rampage at the Washington Navy Yard, where a shooter who claimed to hear voices in his head killed 12 people, as well as physical pain, projections of UFOs and targeted childhood cancers. Could this be possible? Since HAARP is very real, we know a great deal about what it does. But much of this

The conspiracy theories about HAARP took off thanks to a combination of timing and the people involved with building it. HAARP began operations in 1993, and it took a few more years for the first conspiracy theories about what it 'really' does to hit the media. In 1995, Nick Begich, Jr, the son of an Alaskan congressman, published a book called *Angels Don't Play This HAARP: Advances in Tesla Technology*, making a series of wild accusations. Begich claimed that the array can 'disrupt human mental processes, jam all global communications systems, change weather patterns over large areas, interfere with wildlife migration patterns, negatively affect your health, [and] unnaturally impact the earth's upper atmosphere.' Begich goes on and on describing how HAARP will be used to 'boil the upper atmosphere', 'alter mental functions' and even fry the nervous systems of America's enemies, creating what Begich refers to as 'war without death'.

The book took off in the nascent internet conspiracy movement and among listeners to Art Bell's popular conspiracy radio show *Coast to Coast AM*, and Begich sold over 100,000 copies. There is now conspiracy media all over the internet accusing HAARP of controlling our weather and creating massive superstorms, including strengthening Hurricane Sandy to help Barack Obama get re-elected; of causing and targeting earthquakes against nations that run afoul of the United States; of sending ELF waves bouncing off mobile phone towers for the purposes of tracking our calls and movements; of causing California's recent spate of fires and drought; and even of targeting individual people for harassment through physical and mental pain.

It's also spiralled out into parallel conspiracy theories. One of the most cited is that HAARP was actually developed to harvest natural gas and superheat it into a focused, high-energy beam that could vaporize everything from incoming missiles to enemy cities. Another is that the Russian military believed that HAARP could 'trigger a cascade of electrons that could flip Earth's magnetic poles'. It's also linked to chemtrails, UFOs, the coming of the Antichrist and a variety of mostly psychosomatic diseases.

A RESEARCH STATION THAT WASN'T EVEN RESEARCHING

So is any of this true? HAARP has so many claims made about it and against it that debunking them all would involve a book as long as *Angels Don't Play This HAARP*. Begich claims that the array is an extension of the incredibly advanced research that Nikola Tesla did near the end of his life, on topics like electronic power transmission, free energy and horrific weapons like death rays and scalar bubbles – work confiscated by the FBI, never to be made public. It's true that much of Tesla's final work was examined by the FBI (by a physicist uncle of Donald Trump, no less), but that work was found to be mostly delusional self-promotion. Tesla was penniless and likely battling advanced mental

illness when he died – and none of the fantastical research he supposedly pioneered in those final days was ever tested or even completed.

Beyond invoking Tesla, a good clue that a conspiracy theory is just a conspiracy theory is that it involves numerous different people making numerous different accusations about the same thing. They can't all be true, and if they can't all be true, why would one be true and another not true? A machine that could control weather *and* fault lines *and* human brains *and* storms would be a scientific marvel on a par with the wheel or fire. But HAARP doesn't have the capability to do any of that, and despite accusations about it being developed by various nefarious actors (usually pegged as the ARCO oil company or the US government's weapons research arm DARPA), it's far less powerful than conspiracy theories would suggest.

HAARP is composed of an observatory and an 11-hectare field with 180 high frequency antennae, each one 22 m (72 ft) tall, and with 3,600 kilowatts of transmission power. Essentially, these are more powerful mobile phone towers. They can send low frequency radio signals, create a weak aurora that's barely visible at night and slightly heat up parts of the upper atmosphere. ELF waves are useful for passing information through seawater or around the Earth, but at such a low data transmission rate that they're useless for anything other than basic communication. They have no ability to do the fantastical things conspiracy theorists ascribe to them, and while exposure to ELF waves has been found to create slight irritation in test subjects, the power needed to do anything more than make someone close by itch would be enormous and impractical.

There's also the matter of HAARP having been closed from 2013 to 2015 due to a lack of funding, after the Air Force decided it wasn't getting its money's worth. And yet, superstorms, earthquakes and headaches all kept happening while HAARP was closed. Fortunately, the University of Alaska Fairbanks acquired HAARP from the Air Force in 2015, reopening it as a scientific research facility open to scientists from around the world, and conducting dozens of experiments each year. And some even use ELF waves.

But even with all that context, HAARP has become a conspiracy theorist catch-all, something they can easily blame for whatever they feel like needs to be blamed on something. The truth is far less interesting – but more accurate.

re they a measure of convenience or an instrument of control? A handy means of tracking valuable items or a nefarious method of surveilling humans? These are the questions that surround Radio Frequency Identification (RFID) chips, small data storage devices that are activated by the radio waves of the device used to track them. About the size of a grain of rice, RFID chips have existed since the early 1970s, and are used for everything from automatic toll collection to supply chain management and tracking livestock to passport control.

Because of their passive energy use, they don't need their own power source, such as a battery. This allows them to be made cheaply, sold in bulk and disposed of easily. And they fit neatly into all sorts of tags, cards and labels. But it's exactly their use for tracking and cataloguing that has put RFID chips at the centre of a nefarious conspiracy theory, one that taps into our deepest fears about surveillance and identity: mandatory RFID chipping of humans for the purposes of tracking, and maybe even herding. After all, if they can track cows and packages, why not humans? Some Christian fundamentalists even see the mandatory insertion of RFID chips as a 21st-century version of the biblical 'mark of the beast', a conspiracy theory previously reserved for barcodes.

Putting aside all of the conspiracies, there are real concerns about the safety and privacy of RFID chips, sparking an entire industry of 'RFID-blockers' that will supposedly foil thieves from secretly scanning the

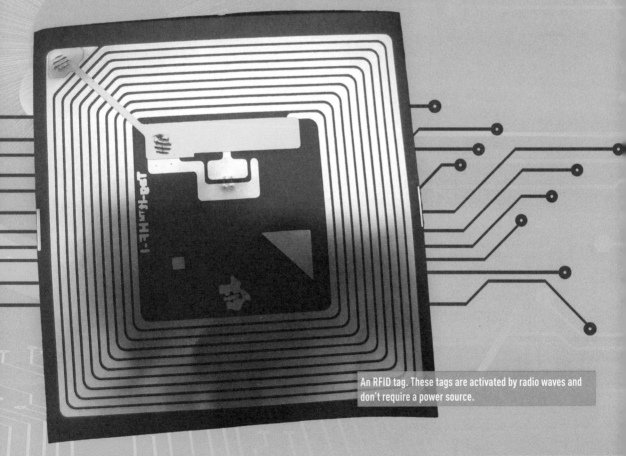

An RFID tag. These tags are activated by radio waves and don't require a power source.

chips in your credit cards or pulling your passport information without your consent. And of course, anything that can be used to track people can also be manipulated into spying on them and collecting data. So are RFID chips really a sinister way for the powers that be to track and control our movements? Or just a technology with a lot of uses that we should probably spend less time worrying about?

THE MARK OF THE BEAST

It's almost impossible to separate RFID chip conspiracy theories from their biblical connotations – that their mandatory implanting fulfils the mark of the beast written of in the Revelation of John, heralding the end of the world. Citing the need for Christians to 'consider the industry plans' of RFID use, including 'tracking people around stores, following their movements in public and even spying on them in their homes', the authors of the 2006 book *The Spychips Threat* call on followers of Christ to reject this technology as invasive and ungodly. At the same time, many Orthodox Jews reject RFID technology as a form of 'numbering', which is forbidden in the Old Testament. There are even comparisons by both Jews and Christians to Nazi-era tattooing and marking of Jews, with *The Spychips Threat* authors rhetorically asking 'What if Hitler had RFID?'

The fear behind mandatory chip implantation doesn't just have religious connotations. Privacy experts and libertarians have long argued that at some point, humans will be commonly implanted with RFID chips, giving everyone from our employers to the government the ability to track us. Several American companies already use fitness trackers to log employee physical activity. Is it any wonder that conspiracy theorists see such danger in RFID tracking? A number of conspiracy theories claimed that the United States' massive healthcare overhaul Obamacare would lead to anyone seeking government-run healthcare to be RFID chipped. Indeed, a deeply buried provision of the law required that a 'device be implanted in the majority of people who opt to become covered by the public healthcare option', though it only applied to the Department of Health and Human Services creating a registry to track the use of medical devices. Nonetheless, such rumours about mandatory chipping to facilitate a liberal healthcare law flew during the Clinton and Obama administrations alike.

Finally, there are the sad stories of those who see themselves as 'targeted individuals', innocent people attacked with powerful and secret electronic weapons as test subjects in non-consensual experiments, carried out to test the capabilities of their latest gadgets. TIs, as they call themselves, believe they have been randomly singled out for 'touchless torture', a kind of remote cruelty encompassing everything from electronic harassment to intense physical pain and mind control. And it's coordinated through secretly implanted RFID chips, placed by the government without their consent

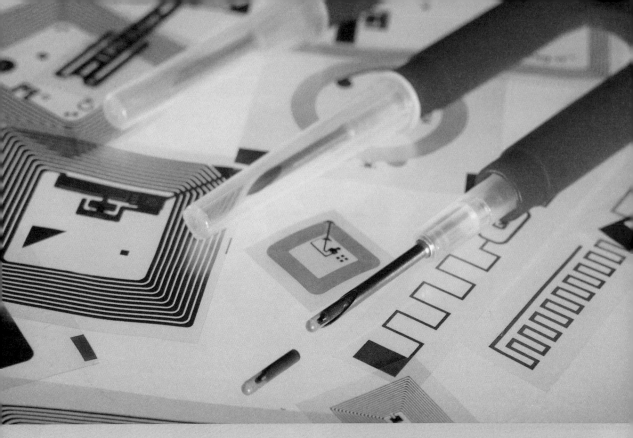

to help target their torture. While uncommon, this is a real phenomenon, with real victims. Websites catering to TIs are full of tips for how to find and disable the RFID chips they've been violated with, theoretically making it harder for the government to target them – yet even that usually doesn't stop the torture.

OLD CONCERNS MADE NEW AGAIN

Like many new and suddenly omnipresent technologies, it's hard to separate the actual concerns about the safety and security of RFID chips from the supposed horrors of mandatory tracking and touchless torture. Before the idea of mandatory RFID chips spurred 'mark of the beast' comparisons, Christian millennialists were complaining that we'd all be the subject of mandatory barcodes tattooed on our bodies so that the forces of evil could track and herd us. And before that, Social Security numbers were seen as the US government attaching us with the mark of the beast. In fact, there are stories of fundamentalist Christians going to court after being terminated from jobs for refusing to provide their Social Security number – with legal penalties attached to employers who don't report them.

The stories behind 'targeted individuals', while based on real suffering, fundamentally misunderstand how RFID technology works, as the reader must be

extremely close to the chip to activate it. While the pain and fear these people express are very real, none of it has ever been proven to have originated from a secret government weapon. Generally speaking, a set of vague and ever-changing maladies with no clear cause or evidence are signs not of electronic attack, but of a psychosomatic illness that can be treated with talk therapy and medication. And much of the 'contactless' payment technology utilizing RFID chips proved unwieldy or unpopular, and was supplanted by payment apps and QR codes. RFID chips are standard on US passports, but they have weak signal capabilities that can only be activated at close range, and RFID credit cards never took off, with the vast majority of credit cards using EMV technology that can only be run through specific readers. But the paranoia is real enough that a number of states have passed laws against theoretical mandatory chipping, while others have banned RFID skimming technology, despite no evidence that any financial crimes have ever been committed through surreptitious scanning of RFID chips.

RFID tracking has legitimate uses, including

making sure children get on and off school buses, ensuring the safety of memory-addled residents at nursing homes and replacing fraud-prone employee timeclock technology. Meanwhile, products to block or disrupt RFID signals are big business, despite their having no real use or proof of efficacy. It's frightening to think of the government mandating that we be tagged with tracking devices, but it's clear that such an idea is a flight of paranoia, and not a necessary solution to any real problem.

A Greek nun protests against RFID chips. Christian millennialists see the RFID chips as the 'mark of the beast'.

The 'chemtrails' conspiracy theory is one of the most mainstream and widely believed on the internet. Its believers think that the governments of the world are using commercial aircraft to spray long paths of unknown chemical substances in the air for a wide variety of purposes, speculating on everything from weather warfare to population control. They claim that the proof is right above our heads. Just look up on a sunny day, and you're likely to see a jet plane with a white line behind it. Some of the clouds dissipate easily, while others seem to hang in the air for long periods of time, with little rhyme or reason.

The technical term for these long aerial paths is 'contrails' – a contraction of 'condensation' and 'trails' that simply denotes the path of ice crystals left behind when hot exhaust from a jet engine hits the cold air of

A CONSPIRACY FOR THE INTERNET AGE

One reason it has become so embedded in modern conspiracy culture is that it took off at the same time as the internet itself: the mid-1990s.

A 1996 report entitled 'Weather as a Force Multiplier: Owning the Weather in 2025' presented hypothetical strategies for how the American military could control the weather for war-fighting purposes – providing frightening possibilities with concerning names such as 'Decrease Comfort Level/Morale', 'Induce Drought', and 'Storm Enhancement'. The delivery system for these horror weapons would include 'clouds made of smart particles' and 'injection of chemical vapours'. It didn't take long for the nascent

the atmosphere. In fact, there is no evidence that this is not what chemtrails actually are, and an enormous amount of evidence that proves contrails are what we think they are.

And yet, the chemtrails conspiracy theory has reached the mainstream. Multiple YouTube videos offering 'proof' of their existence have over one million views, while dozens of books and thousands of articles have been written about their supposed evils. If one simply looks at the sky, it's easy enough to see the long trails, crisscrossing and smearing all over what would normally be beautiful blue sky and wonder what's really going on.

So what is really going on?

internet conspiracy movement to take these admittedly frightening concepts and develop its own theories about what the government was really doing. The long trails left by high-flying planes looked exactly what it might look like if the government was actually putting these tactics into action – despite an Air University report making it clear that as of its writing 'artificial weather technologies do not currently exist'.

Multiple government agencies leapt to action to debunk the growing conspiracy theory using fact sheets and research reports, but this only fuelled the fire of distrust, given that it was essentially the very people carrying out weather warfare trying to convince us that weather warfare was not real. Why wouldn't they? And so, the belief that they were spraying us in order to use our weather against us only grew stronger.

A tornado rips across the landscape. An American military report from 1996 described the possibility of using the weather as a weapon.

But like most conspiracy theories, even the alternate explanation for what contrails are (i.e. weather modification weapons) had alternate explanations. Some posited that the chemicals are actually a form of mind control, ensuring we're pliable to the brainwashing of the government and mass media and making us too lethargic to fight back. Others claim they're designed for general 'health erosion', making us sick so that Big Pharma can sell us cures for our man-made diseases – a perfect circle of decrepitude and greed. Blocking the sun, creating earthquakes, suppressing evolution, mass genetic modification of food, infesting our bodies with 'nano-fibres', and even carrying out genocide are all the supposed reasons for the government to spray our air with chemicals.

Believers in the chemtrail conspiracy present a variety of pictures and videos as evidence that they claim are smoking guns. A few that have made the rounds on social media include multiple pictures of 'chemtrails tanks' inside aeroplanes (further research showed that these were only the ballast tanks used for testing the effects of passengers moving around during a flight), along with Photoshop-edited graphics and pictures of actual cloud formations that have simply been mislabelled.

THE SCIENCE OF CHEMTRAILS
In the case of chemtrails, the 'official story' seems the most plausible, based as it is on the bedrock of established science. Contrails form when hot gases from a jet engine hit the cold air of the upper atmosphere. The water vapour freezes very quickly after being emitted, combines with particles of dust or smoke, and forms a visible haze of microscopic ice crystals trailing behind the aeroplane. But the effect isn't instantaneous, which is why there's always a gap between the aeroplane and the contrail behind it.

Water ballast tanks on board a Boeing 747. These tanks are often mistaken by conspiracy theorists for barrels containing chemtrails.

Eventually, that trail of ice crystals either melts or smears as it dissipates – the reason why some contrails disappear fairly quickly, and others can linger for much longer, smearing into any number of shapes. It's entirely dependent on air temperature, humidity and wind. This effect is even visible on the ground. Just breathe out on a cold day. Hot water vapour leaves your mouth, and when it hits the cold air, it begins to freeze – hence the steam we breathe out when it's cold.

We've known about chemtrails for far longer than the conspiracy theory itself has been around. There are dozens of pictures of fleets of World War II bombers leaving contrails behind them, as well as newsreel footage of bucolic English country scenes dotted with the contrails of dogfighting aircraft above them during the Battle of Britain. Were they actually spraying weather modification chemicals on the enemy?

Even if there was an actual evil plot to use commercial jets to spray us with chemicals, using high-flying jets would be the least-efficient and least-effective way to carry it out. A thin chemical strand sprayed out by one plane miles above us would dissipate harmlessly and never reach us. You'd need to use fleets of crop dusters to spray people with chemicals in order to control our minds or infest us with fibres.

And who is flying these planes? Who is equipping them with these horrific chemicals? Who is giving the orders denoting what gets sprayed when and where? Are the passengers aware? The flight attendants?

Nobody seems to have any answers to these simple questions.

And if the 'chemicals' are meant to modify our weather, nobody has bothered to test the atmosphere for their effects. Because nobody agrees on what they are, there can't be tests for them. But just to be safe, a group of 77 actual atmospheric scientists, many of whom are experts in how chemicals interact with high altitude, dug through the 'evidence', then published a report in the high-impact, peer-reviewed journal *Environmental Research Letters*. Of those 77 scientists, 76 stated that they had found no evidence of what they defined as a 'secret large-scale atmospheric programme.' They deduced that everything we know about contrails can easily be explained by basic science and how the atmosphere works.

The chemtrail conspiracy is vague, nebulous and hard to prove. It will likely linger on the internet for a long time, but it is safe to say that we can rest assured that we aren't being poisoned, enslaved or threatened by contrails. They might look sinister, but they're really just science.

A sign warns about the dangers of chemtrails in Australia.

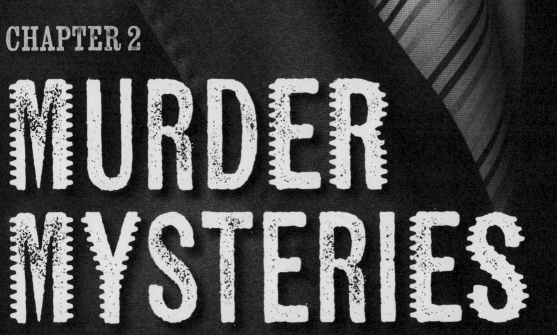

CHAPTER 2

MURDER MYSTERIES

From Agatha Christie's genteel criminals, to the more graphic detective novels of the twenty-first century, a good murder mystery is the book of choice with which to curl up in an armchair for millions of people the world over. And if that murder mystery involves celebrities, sex, politicians, and may in fact be true, that only serves to make it all the more enjoyable!

WHO SHOT JFK?

The assassination of John F. Kennedy on 22 November 1963 has generated more conspiracy theories than almost any other crime in history. This is partly because the crime was such a shocking, dramatic event. As we all know, the president was fatally shot in full view of the public while riding along in an open-topped motorcade, with his wife beside him. But it is also because the hastily assembled Warren Commission, set up just one week after the assassination for the purpose of enquiring

into what happened, failed to account for the many perplexing aspects of the crime. The Commission found that a lone gunman, Lee Harvey Oswald, had fired three shots at the president. The first of these missed the motorcade; the second wounded both Kennedy and the Governor of Texas, John B. Connally, who was also riding in the limousine; and the third and final shot hit Kennedy in the head, killing him.

The related conspiracy theories became known as 'The Lone Gunman Theory' and 'The Single Bullet Theory' (often jokingly referred to as 'The Magic Bullet Theory' because it seemed so unlikely that one bullet could penetrate two people). In time, both theories came to be regarded as highly implausible – not only by the experts but by the majority of the American public, who were polled on numerous occasions in order to obtain their opinions on the matter.

To compound the confusions, on 24 November 1963 Jack Ruby, a Dallas nightclub owner, shot Oswald dead while he was in police captivity. Once again,

the killing took place in full view of the public. The event prompted a new wave of speculation. How was it that Ruby had found it so easy to flout the tight security surrounding Oswald? Had Oswald been swiftly executed in order to prevent incriminating evidence being brought against establishment figures at the trial? And what about Ruby's links to the world of organized crime? Was the Mafia involved in some way with Kennedy's death? Ruby swore that he had been acting on his own, in revenge for the killing, but many disbelieved him. By the time he died of a stroke on 3 January 1967, his motives were still thought by some to be questionable.

THE GRASSY KNOLL

Rumours about the Kennedy assassination persisted throughout the years that followed until, in 1976, the evidence was re-examined by a House Select Committee that was convened for that purpose. This time, the committee found that there were probably two gunmen, not one, and that four bullets were fired: three by Oswald, and one from an unknown gunman hiding in a nearby area that was known as the Grassy Knoll. Many witness reports were collected, some of them conflicting, and evidence was also acquired from people who had photographed, filmed, or recorded the event. However, the report was not conclusive. It merely

LEFT: The most famous conspiracy of all: President John F. Kennedy and wife Jackie in the limousine that would take Kennedy to his death on Dealey Plaza, Dallas.

BELOW: First Lady Jacqueline Kennedy leans over to assist her husband who lies on the rear of the car after being shot.

The Texas Book Depository offers a clear line of sight to the street which the presidential motorcade passed through.

The Carcano rifle used by Lee Harvey Oswald. Oswald was a trained marksman, who could be expected to hit a target just 88 yards away.

suggested that a conspiracy of some kind seemed likely, given the probability that two gunmen were responsible (a theory based on acoustic recordings of the gunshots fired).

A CASE OF FOUL PLAY?

After the assassination, many troubling facts surrounding the event came to light. For example, the limousine that the president had been travelling in was taken away and cleaned up directly after the shooting, rather than being preserved so that forensic examinations could take place. Also, Kennedy's body should have been inspected by the local coroner according to Texan law, but it was immediately taken to Washington instead. Moreover, the area in which the assassination had taken place, the Dealey Plaza, should have been sealed off by police. The place where Oswald worked, the Texas School Book Depository, should have been closed off also. However, in the event neither place was secured, so vital clues to what really happened might well have been lost. And later, important pieces of evidence were found to be missing, such as the hat that Governor Connally was holding in his hand when he was shot, and the cufflink from his shirt. More shockingly, photographs of Kennedy's autopsy also disappeared.

Much of this could be put down to official incompetence but, after the assassination, there were so many anomalies surrounding the event that a host of conspiracy theories arose to explain what had actually happened. Some of these – like the idea that Kennedy masterminded his own suicide – are difficult to credit. Others, however, such as the theory that right-wing elements of the American establishment wanted Kennedy out of the way, and therefore arranged the shooting, do not seem altogether implausible.

THE RIVAL STRIKES

One of the most compelling theories regarding the assassination of Kennedy concerns his political role. At the time, the Cold War had preserved an uneasy truce between the two superpowers, the USA and the USSR, and many thought that it played an essential part in preserving the status quo and preventing nuclear war. In some quarters, Kennedy was seen as a loose cannon, a young idealistic president who could not be relied upon to maintain a strong stance in the face of Soviet aggression. The Cuban Missile Crisis, in which the USSR and the USA had come close to an all-out nuclear conflict, had shown how important it was to maintain a balance between the two sides and what the consequences of any change in the status quo might be.

American foreign policy at the time – which later turned out to be disastrous – was to escalate America's 'anti-communist' involvement in Vietnam. Kennedy had shown signs of pulling back from the conflict by recalling United States forces and questioning the scale of human losses that would inevitably ensue. Thus, Kennedy was beginning to be seen as a liability within the political establishment. Conversely, his vice president, Lyndon B. Johnson, appeared to offer a safe pair of hands. He was older, more pragmatic and

apparently impervious to the liberal currents running through America during the 1960s.

When Johnson took over, he immediately sent troops back to Vietnam and stepped up anti-communist political propaganda in the United States. The speedy change in foreign and domestic policy confirmed to some observers that the political establishment was behind Kennedy's killing. Oswald was thought to be a decoy figure, a pro-communist who had been hired to shoot the president so that Johnson could take over. The extent of Johnson's personal involvement in the plot remained unclear, but some believed that he had arranged the shooting himself. It also transpired that shortly before he died Kennedy had been thinking of removing Johnson from office, mainly because the vice president was the subject of four criminal investigations (all of which were dropped after he became the new president). Johnson had more than enough motive to arrange the assassination, it seemed.

MAFIA MADNESS

Another theory was that President Kennedy was killed by the Mafia. The Kennedy regime had made it a priority to crack down on organized crime and high-level Mafia leaders were being prosecuted for illegal activities such as gambling, drug running, racketeering and pimping. There was particular resentment among some Mafia bosses, as they had directed Mafia-linked organizations, such as workers' unions, to run campaigns supporting Kennedy's election. Because they expected to be protected

Newspaper report from 24 November 1963 of the *San Francisco Examiner* with an article on the arrest of Lee Harvey Oswald.

Police Say They Have the Killer

San Francisco Examiner

AMERICA FIRST

MONARCH OF THE DAILIES

SUNDAY, NOVEMBER 24, 1963   220 PAGES   3CH

Sen. Engle at White House--First Public Appearance

A Stunned Nation Mourns

Capital's Somber Mood

Business Halts

ASSASSINATION SUSPECT LEE HARVEY OSWALD
Police say photos are tightening the noose

Murder Gun Linked To Accused Assassin

Editor's Report
An American

He Is Still Defiant

from prosecution once he was in power, so the theory goes, Kennedy's war on organized crime was seen as a betrayal and so he was gunned down in revenge.

It was significant that Jack Ruby, who shot Oswald, had worked for Al Capone as a young man and had continued to be part of the world of organized crime.

According to this theory, Oswald was hired to shoot the president so that it would seem that a communist had done the deed. Oswald was then shot by Ruby, who was posing as a loyal citizen. In this way, Oswald's testimony would not be heard and it would not emerge that it was the Mafia, and not the communists, who had shot one of America's most popular presidents.

Finally, commentators noted that prosecutions of Mafia organizations returned to their normal level after the assassination of Kennedy.

A CIA PLOT?

Not only the Mafia but the CIA had strong reasons to get Kennedy out of the way. Once in office, Kennedy infuriated the agency by refusing to back the Bay of Pigs invasion in Cuba, which was part of a plot to overthrow the Communist leader Fidel Castro. Kennedy sacked the director of the CIA, Alan Dulles, and there were constant run-ins between the president and the agency, especially after the failed invasion of Cuba.

The CIA worked very closely with the Mafia, and both organizations saw it as mutually beneficial to oust Castro from Cuba. The CIA's motive was to rid the United States of their closest communist neighbour and the Mafia's motive was to win back control of the organized crime business in Cuba, which they had quickly lost when Castro took control.

Several top Mafia men, aided by the CIA, plotted to assassinate Castro. Thus, Kennedy's perceived reluctance to support their anti-Cuban stance was a constant source of irritation to the CIA and the Mafia.

THE FBI BOSS

The head of the FBI, J. Edgar Hoover, was also suspected of plotting Kennedy's assassination. There was a good deal of mutual animosity between Hoover and the Kennedy clan. Hoover and Johnson, on the other hand, were the best of friends. Hoover was coming up to retirement age and he knew that Kennedy would let him go whereas Johnson, by contrast, would keep him

in. Commentators noted that after Johnson became president, he did indeed retain Hoover's services as head of the FBI – 'for life'.

THE OTHER CONTENDERS

There are many other theories regarding the culprits in the Kennedy assassination: some of them simple, others labyrinthine. First, there are the 'economic issue' conspiracy theories. For example, some think that the oil barons wanted the president dead because he had changed the tax laws regarding oil, which would lose them enormous profits. Others suppose that officials of the US central bank, the Federal Reserve, were worried by the president's plans to stop the counterfeiting of money by backing the currency with precious metals.

Then there are the 'political issue' hypotheses. Castro was behind the assassination, it has been said, as a response to the constant attempts by United States agents to murder him. Another theory is that followers of the South Vietnam president, Ngo Dinh Diem, ordered the assassination in revenge for his death after the United States plotted a coup against him. Others say that Kennedy was a puppet of the Soviet Union, which then turned against him.

The following theories are more implausible, in the eyes of most people. The first one states that Kennedy was killed in order to avenge the honour of Jacqueline

Jackie Kennedy with her second husband Aristotle Onassis. The more outlandish conspiracy theories name both of them as potential culprits in the assassination of JFK.

Kennedy, to whom he had been unfaithful on many occasions. Another suggests that Aristotle Onassis ordered Kennedy's murder, along with his friends in the secret Illuminati cabal. Finally, some people imagine that Kennedy did not die at all, but that the whole event was somehow stage-managed to look as though he did. To support this theory, an exchange of bodies would need to have taken place at the autopsy.

Whatever the truth of the matter, some people consider that the Warren Commission's initial findings were questionable and that there were strong pressures to rid the country of a president that threatened to shake up the status quo, both within the government and outside it. Perhaps President Kennedy acted through inexperience and recklessness, as some critics believed, or maybe he had made a serious moral commitment to rid the US of the atmosphere of distrust and fear that had built up as a result of the Cold War, both in terms of domestic and of foreign policy.

For many, Kennedy's death was seen as a tragedy. Whatever his personal failings, he stood as a symbol of hope for a better, more peaceable world, not only for America but for many other countries too. On the day he was killed there were hundreds of troops flying back from Vietnam on his express orders. Had he gone on to withdraw entirely from Vietnam, the Vietnamese and the American public might have been spared one of the most appalling wars in recent history. No wonder, then, that so many intelligent, committed political analysts refuse to let the matter drop and continue to ask to this day: who shot JFK?

The Warren Commission, set up a few days after the assassination, concluded that Oswald, and only Oswald, was responsible for killing Kennedy.

THE ASSASSINATION OF MALCOLM X

A t the time of his assassination on 21 February 1965, Malcolm X was one of the two leading black political figures in America. The other was Martin Luther King, who was himself assassinated just a couple of years later. However, where Martin Luther King was a broadly popular figure, a man of the Church with a commitment to non-violent change, Malcolm was seen as a much more threatening figure. White liberals hailed Martin Luther King as the leader of the civil rights movement. On the other hand, Malcolm X was treated with suspicion because he was the main spokesman for a group called the Nation of Islam – commonly known as the Black Muslims – who were overtly anti-white and rather less inclined to turn the other cheek.

During the early sixties, Malcolm, a former petty criminal who had discovered the Nation of Islam while in prison, became a hate figure in the mainstream American media and was routinely vilified for his anti-white statements.

During the last year of his life, however, he began to travel more, especially to Africa, and after meeting anti-apartheid activists in South Africa he became convinced that black and white people could work together to achieve political change. This realization caused him to split with the Nation of Islam and during the summer of 1964 he formed his own group, the Organization of Afro-American Unity.

Shortly after forming this organization Malcolm X returned to Africa for a period of several months, finally returning to the United States in November 1964. While he was in Africa he continually complained that he was being followed by CIA agents. In Cairo he was seriously ill, perhaps as the result of having his food poisoned. Things were no better when he returned to the United States. Over the next few months a feud developed between Malcolm and the Nation of Islam, the group he had resigned from. Death threats were issued against him.

HOUSE FIREBOMBED

A week before his eventual assassination Malcolm's house in Queens, New York was firebombed. At the time Malcolm assumed that the Nation of Islam was behind the attack. The following day, 15 February, Malcolm made a speech at the Audubon Ballroom in Harlem. As he spoke a scuffle broke out in the audience. Six days later Malcolm returned to the Audubon. Mysteriously, all the other speakers that were scheduled to appear cancelled their engagements. While Malcolm was waiting to speak he allegedly confided to friends in the backstage area that he was not sure that it had been the Nation of Islam after all that had been behind the firebombing. Then he went onstage and began to give his speech.

At around 3.05 p.m. Eastern Standard Time a disturbance broke out in the crowd of 400. A man yelled, 'Get your hand outta my pocket! Don't be messin' with my pockets!' Then a smoke bomb went off at the back of the auditorium, causing confusion. Malcolm's bodyguards moved forward to calm the crowd but meanwhile, taking advantage of the chaos, a black man came towards the stage and shot Malcolm in the chest at point-blank range with a sawn-off shotgun.

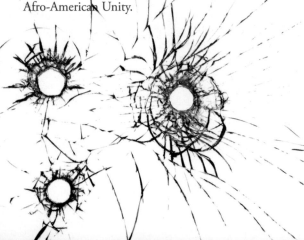

Malcolm X recognized the immense power of the press and used it assiduously in promoting himself and his organization the Nation of Islam.

Malcolm X returning home on the 14 February 1965 after his house was firebombed. There were many suspects for the crime, but nothing was ever proven in court.

Two other men quickly charged towards the stage and fired handguns at Malcolm. The three assassins attempted to escape, but the angry crowd managed to capture one of the two men with handguns, one Talmadge Hayer.

Malcolm's bodyguard Gene Roberts, actually an undercover cop, attempted to resuscitate him but to no avail. Malcolm was dead. The autopsy was performed by New York City's Chief Medical Examiner, Dr Milton Helpern, and it was discovered that 'the cause of death was multiple shotgun pellet and bullet wounds in the chest, heart and aorta'. Malcolm had been hit by eight shotgun slugs and nine bullets.

Malcolm's funeral was held in Harlem on 27 February 1965 at the Faith Temple Church of God in Christ (now Child's Memorial Temple Church of God in Christ). The ceremony was attended by 1,500 people. Malcolm X was buried at the Ferncliff Cemetery in Hartsdale, New York, where his friends took the shovels away from the waiting gravediggers and buried him themselves. Soon, three people were arrested for his murder. They were Nation of Islam members Talmadge Hayer, Norman 3X Butler, and Thomas 15X Johnson. All three were convicted of

first-degree murder in March 1966.

On the face of it, this was an open and shut case, the result of infighting between black radicals. The Nation of Islam had murdered their greatest ex-member. The mainstream media either said good riddance or shed crocodile tears. And moved on. Gradually, though, suspicions began to circulate that all may not have been as it seemed.

A COVER-UP?

Suspicion centred around the notion that Malcolm might have been murdered by his fellow black men who had been manipulated: they could have believed that they were carrying out the wishes of the Nation of Islam.

It was not hard to find fuel for those suspicions. Even in the immediate aftermath of the murder a police source had told the *Herald Tribune* that 'several' members of the highly secretive Bureau of Special Services (BOSS) were present in the audience at the time of the killing. One of those undercover cops, Gene Roberts, was one of Malcolm X's bodyguards at the time he was killed.

The bullet holes from the shooting of Malcolm X at the Audubon Ballroom have been circled by the police, 1965.

Talmadge Hayer was convicted for the murder of Malcolm X and claimed that he was the only one involved.

On 25 February 1965, four days after the assassination of Malcolm X, one of his senior lieutenants at the OAAU, Leon 4X Ameer, announced that he was convinced that his life was in danger. Less than three weeks later, he died of an apparent overdose of sleeping pills. It is alleged that he had been on the point of revealing evidence of government involvement in Malcolm's murder.

Further speculation surrounds the question of who really carried out the killing. Talmadge Hayer was certainly guilty, but there is plenty of evidence to suggest that his co-defendants were not even at the Audubon Ballroom at the time, and that the two other killers have never been brought to justice. As for Talmadge Hayer, he has stated that he was not a member of the Nation of Islam and 'that the man who hired him was not a Muslim' either, according to a 1971 book, *The Assassination of Malcolm X*.

So was it the government or the Nation of Islam that was really behind the murder? There is a suspicion of government involvement here, and it is probably true to say that few people at the FBI shed many tears for Malcolm X. On the other hand, the Nation of Islam was locked in a struggle with Malcolm and its leading lights like Elijah Muhammad, and his eventual successor Louis Farrakhan did publicly call for Malcolm's elimination. It might well be that both parties are implicated. Perhaps the killers were Black Muslims and they were egged on by agents provocateurs. Whatever the truth behind the killing, the inescapable fact is that another great sixties leader was cut down in his prime, like John F. Kennedy before him and Martin Luther King not long afterwards.

THE DEATH OF PRINCESS OF

DIANA WAS S
IN A CAR CRASH D
SHE PASSED AWAY
AT DAWN.

Diana pictured in 1996, the year before her death. She was relentlessly pursued by the paparazzi from the time of her marriage to the Prince of Wales in 1981.

DIANA, WALES

In the early hours of Sunday, 31 August 1997, news of the death of Diana, Princess of Wales shocked the world. She and her lover Dodi Al-Fayed had been killed in a car crash as they sped through a Paris tunnel during the night. The driver of the car, Henri Paul, was also killed and Diana's bodyguard, Trevor Rees Jones, was seriously injured.

At first, the cause of the accident seemed straight-forward enough. In an attempt to shake off the paparazzi who were pursuing the couple on motorcycles, the driver had taken the car down into the tunnel just a little too fast and had ended up smacking into one of the pillars inside it. But then, questions began to be asked. Why was the car travelling so fast? Had Henri Paul been drinking? If so, why had he been allowed to drive the car of Britain's number one celebrity, Diana, whose doomed marriage to the heir to the throne, Prince Charles, had generated pages of speculation and scandal in the worldwide press for over a decade. Why had the lights in the tunnel, and the security cameras, apparently failed just before the crash? Why had it taken so long for Diana, who was still alive after the crash, to be taken to hospital by ambulance?

And, after her death from cardiac arrest in the hospital, why was her body immediately embalmed, before a post-mortem could be undertaken? Had she been pregnant? Was it possible that MI6 and the British royal family wanted her – and her lover, son of one of Britain's richest businessmen, Mohammed Al-Fayed – out of the way? Had the Princess's indiscretions – her affairs, her criticism of the royal family, her increasingly eccentric behaviour – earned her enemies in high places? Al-Fayed senior claimed that the couple had been murdered, that they had been planning to marry and that the British establishment had decided that it was time to get them out of the way.

At first, Al-Fayed's claim was seen as paranoid but as time went on and more anomalies in the case surfaced, the theory began to seem less outlandish. Soon, others began to be convinced that this was no ordinary accident but a case of foul play.

DID MI6 KILL DIANA?

Initially, the press reported the tragic event as a car crash caused by the fact that Henri Paul, the driver, had simply made a mistake. But it then began to emerge that Paul, a security officer at the Ritz hotel, was an experienced and careful driver who had taken driving courses in the past. Not only this, but the car was only travelling at about 60–70 mph (96–112 kph), not at

120 mph (193 kph) as had at first been reported. Next, there were allegations that Paul had been drunk at the wheel, but security cameras at the hotel showed that he was acting in a perfectly normal way minutes before taking the wheel. Moreover, he was unlikely to have been drinking when on call to such important hotel guests as Diana and Dodi Al-Fayed. Later, it was found that even before they took samples of his blood the police had in fact announced that Paul was drunk.

So, if the car was not going too fast and Paul was not drunk, why had the accident happened? Conflicting reports by some witnesses told of a car blocking the way so that Paul had to turn off his normal route into the tunnel and of cycles ramming the car as it travelled along, causing it to swerve. Some suggested that Paul had been in the pay of MI6, that he had been hired to kill Diana and Dodi and that something had gone wrong at the last minute so that he ended up killing himself as well. What was odd, and is still unexplained, is why Dodi asked Paul to drive the couple home instead of using his usual driver, Philippe Junot.

THE FATAL MOMENT

According to some reports, all the lights in the tunnel went out shortly before the car approached, and the security cameras in the tunnel also failed. On this evidence, a theory has been constructed that Paul was used as a dupe, and that the French authorities deliberately arranged for the car to crash, thus killing the inmates. It has even been suggested that Rees Jones was somehow in on the plot because he survived, protected by his safety belt when Diana and Dodi were not wearing theirs. However, his involvement is somewhat implausible. Deliberately travelling in a car that is destined to have a fatal accident seems a little too risky a strategy – even for a man trained by the Parachute Regiment, one of the toughest regiments in the British army.

What does emerge as odd, however, is how the French authorities responded at the scene of the accident. In the immediate minutes after the crash, Diana appeared not to be seriously harmed. It later emerged that she was suffering from internal bleeding, but to the off-duty doctor who arrived first on the scene, Frederic Mailliez, she did not appear to be in a fatal condition. As she clearly needed medical attention, an ambulance was called but, strangely, it took it over an hour to get to the hospital. It even stopped on the way for ten minutes! Afterwards, it was explained that the

ambulance had stopped in order to administer a shot of adrenalin to the princess and that it had travelled slowly to avoid jolting her.

However, many remain unconvinced by this and they still cannot understand why Diana was taken to a hospital some distance away, when there were several nearby that could have attended to her. After all, this was no ordinary car crash victim. This was Diana, the Princess of Wales, one of the most famous and recognizable women on the planet.

Not only that, but important evidence was also cleared away from the scene of the accident immediately after the victims had been taken to hospital. Within just a few hours, the tunnel had been cleaned and disinfected and it was soon open to traffic once again. In normal circumstances, one would have expected the authorities to have sealed off the tunnel and have sifted through the evidence in order to find out exactly what had happened. But in this case they did not, which was curious.

THE AFTERMATH

Once Diana had died in hospital, the British royal family reacted oddly to the news. They reportedly sent an emissary to the hospital to retrieve any valuable family jewellery on the body. They then ordered the hospital to embalm the body right away, thus making it impossible for a post-mortem to be carried out. In particular, it was not possible to ascertain whether the princess had been pregnant or not. (She had apparently confided to Doctor Mailliez that she was.) When the press learned of the tragedy, the royal family were roundly condemned for not issuing an official statement and for failing to fly the palace flags at half-mast.

To this day, new theories are still pointing to the possibility that the top ranks of the British establishment joined in a conspiracy to kill Diana, Princess of Wales, because she had not only become an embarrassment to the royal family but also to the state in general. Other theories have also emerged, one of which is that she faked her own death so that she could disappear, thus avoiding the media circus that followed her everywhere she went. Perhaps we will never know the full truth.

What is clear, though, is that the circumstances of her death were not as straightforward as they at first appeared. Also, many of those who dealt with the accident, whether in Britain or in France, were guilty of incompetence, if not murder. In 2005 the official inquiry into Diana's death was reopened in France.

Mohammed Al-Fayed, father of Dodi, looks at the statue that he had commissioned of his dead son and Princess Diana. Mr Al-Fayed is the main proponent of the Diana conspiracy theory.

Diana is loaded – alive – into an ambulance in the Paris underpass. Questions are asked about the length of time the ambulance took to make the journey to the hospital.

John Lennon pictured in 1969 during a 'Bed-in-for-Peace' when he and Yoko Ono used the press attention surrounding their marriage to protest against the Vietnam war.

JOHN LENNON AND THE FBI

When John Lennon was murdered on 8 December 1980, the world reeled in shock. At the time of his death, Lennon was one of the most famous rock stars of all time and after a quiet period away from the public eye he was in the process of returning to the limelight with his first album in five years.

He was shot outside the Dakota Building, where he lived, by a young man named Mark Chapman who was obsessed by his hero and who had a history of mental illness. When Lennon arrived at the building that day with Yoko Ono, Chapman raised a gun and shot the star four times as he tried to run away. Lennon was rushed to hospital but died soon after his arrival. His death was mourned by millions and he continues to be remembered by legions of fans.

The generally accepted view of the murder is that the mentally unstable Chapman acted alone, but there were also those who believed that Lennon was the victim of a conspiracy and that Chapman had in fact acted under orders from a higher authority.

'DANGEROUS EXTREMISTS'

During the late 1960s and the early 1970s, John Lennon had become unpopular with the United States government because of his outspoken criticism of the Vietnam War, among other issues. In a period when the counterculture was at its height, Lennon was seen as one of the most influential figures of the day and he was regarded by the government as highly subversive. J. Edgar Hoover of the FBI noted on Lennon's file that 'all extremists should be considered dangerous'.

As a result of the antagonism that arose between the star and the United States authorities, Lennon was denied permanent residency in America and the administration was constantly looking for ways to deport him. By 1972, Lennon was known to be under surveillance and it was reported that he had spoken about fearing for his life and that of his family. He continued to be monitored by the FBI even when he retired from public life altogether, although less consistently.

Under the Carter administration, the authorities began to take less interest in the politically inactive Lennon, but when President Reagan was elected in 1980 all that changed. It so happened that Lennon emerged from his seclusion just as the new, right-wing administration was beginning to step up its anti-extremist tactics. To some, the fact that Lennon was murdered just a few months after he stepped into the limelight once more was highly significant.

HARD EVIDENCE

Although it is undoubtedly true that Lennon and his wife Yoko Ono were under suspicion from the United States administration for many years, there is a lack of hard evidence to link Mark Chapman to the FBI and the CIA. Several authors have suggested that

John Lennon poses with fan Paul Goresh on 8 December, 1980. Hours later, Lennon would be shot dead by Mark Chapman.

government agencies brainwashed the insecure and mentally fragile Chapman, conducting 'mind control' programmes on him that ordered him to murder John Lennon. However, while there is plenty of documented evidence of Lennon's battle with the United States authorities in the shape of FBI files, those who claim that the government went one step further than mere harassment and had the star shot, using Chapman as the assassin, have very little in the way of facts to back them up. While the accounts of Lennon's constant run-ins with the authorities make fascinating reading – for a time, he was friendly with many of the leading lights of the United States counterculture, such as Jerry Rubin and Abbie Hoffman – it is difficult to see why the government would choose to resolve the conflict by having Lennon murdered. Even if they did, why and how they would have used Chapman to do the deed is another question.

MIND CONTROL

Several commentators have speculated that Chapman was specifically programmed to kill on command. They point to 'Project Bluebird' and 'Project Artichoke', the

CIA's attempts to investigate the possibilities of using scientific methods to control the behaviour of their agents. 'Mind control' experiments were conducted using a number of methods including hypnosis and drugs. Chapman, it is alleged, became a pawn in this game, a 'Manchurian Candidate' who was cold-bloodedly programmed to go out and shoot Lennon for the security services.

Whether or not a person can, in fact, be trained to kill – particularly if this is against their wishes – is questionable. On the other hand, some psychologists have argued that where a subject has a deep-seated desire to kill, and has a specific target in mind, he or she may be encouraged to do so by using various persuasive techniques. This is, of course, especially effective where a subject already has a distorted sense of reality, as in the case of Mark Chapman.

Conspiracy theorists argue that by using a lone drifter with a history of mental illness to commit the murder, the FBI would draw attention away from their own involvement in the crime. However, there are several problems with this theory, apart from the fact that there is so little hard evidence to support

The death of John Lennon at the hands of crazed 'fan' Mark Chapman marked a new intensity of celebrity obsession. Here the London *New Standard* reports on the killing that shocked the world.

it. In particular, it seems unlikely that such a person would make a reliable hit man, to say the least. By the time of his death, John Lennon had made himself very unpopular with the powers that be, both as a result of his political pronouncements and his affiliations to left-wing groups. However, the idea that the CIA or the FBI decided to resolve the situation by programming a mentally unstable gunman to take potshots at him in the middle of New York does seem a little far-fetched.

The fact remains, though, that in 1980 John Lennon was re-emerging from a fallow period to become a public figure once again and that this coincided with a shift towards the right in American politics. Perhaps it was the case that the United States administration feared a re-run of the battles that Lennon had fought with the authorities in the past. Nevertheless, in the absence of hard evidence to link Chapman to the security agencies, it seems more likely that this was sheer coincidence and that, tragically, Lennon met his death just as his star was beginning to rise once more. Perhaps it is harder for many to accept that he was the unfortunate victim of a random killing than that there was a conspiracy to plot his murder.

Could Mark Chapman have been a subject of mind control by the FBI and the CIA?

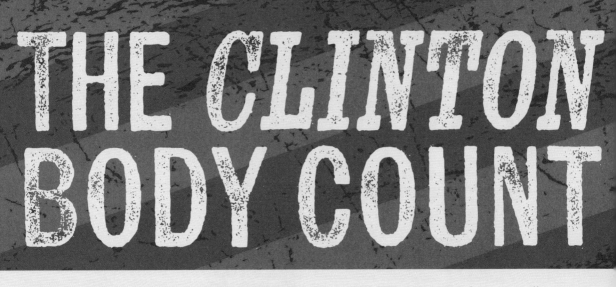

THE CLINTON BODY COUNT

The rise of the anti-government militia movement in the early 1990s in the United States brought with it a conspiracy theory that lives on. Dubbed the 'Clinton Body Count', it's an ever-growing list of people somehow connected to Bill and Hillary Clinton who wound up suffering untimely deaths, either through an unsolved murder, suspicious accident, a fast-moving illness, or a 'suicide' that quite obviously was not self-inflicted.

There are several versions, some of which stretch on for hundreds of names. Some are people who were extremely close to the Clintons, most notably former White House Counsel Vince Foster, who shot himself in the fallout from the scandal that eviscerated the White House Travel Office in 1993. Others had less tangible, but still real, links to the Clintons or their political machine, such as Democratic National Committee members, elected officials, fundraisers or security members.

Yet many others are random lawyers and reporters, or low-level government employees that never had any contact with the president. Some are street hoods from Little Rock. A few haven't even been conclusively proven to exist. And yet, the list continues to grow – even gaining new names in 2018, including a woman who died in a gas explosion in her home who was falsely claimed to be testifying against the Clinton Foundation, and a UN official who died in a weight-lifting accident.

The Clinton Body Count is intensely conspiratorial, rarely evidence-based and driven by leaps in logic that are often simply ludicrous. But it's also not surprising that it took off, given the heavy-handedness with which the Clinton administration took down several militia and anti-government groups, particularly the Branch Davidians compound after a long siege by the FBI.

It's also not as if powerful people don't have the ability to make their enemies disappear. Nor are the Clintons strangers to controversy, conspiracy and even allegedly illegal behaviour. Behaviour that they might want to cover up using the ultimate obscurant – murder. So did they?

Vince Foster, White House Counsel, shot himself in 1993.

Conspiracy theorists accuse Bill and Hillary Clinton of killing a large number of people and covering up their murders.

ORIGINS OF THE LIST

The first version of the Clinton Body Count list was put together by right-wing activist Linda Thompson, a lawyer who quit her job in 1993 to push conspiracy theories. Thompson put it together based on research she'd done for an anti-Clinton film she'd produced, called *Waco: The Big Lie*, which accused Clinton of using ATF agents as hired killers to take out other agents during the Branch Davidians siege.

Thompson compiled the names of two dozen people that she believed had 'died suspiciously and had ties to the Clintons'. She freely admitted she had no actual evidence the Clintons killed these people, relying only on intuition that the media would find more here if it would only bother to dig. The list caught on in far-right American circles, being passed around on text-only BBS sites or via fax.

It made the jump into the mainstream in 1994, thanks to the recently retired arch-conservative California congressman William Dannemeyer, who used Thompson's list as the spine of a letter he sent to Congress urging the body to investigate people in the orbit of the Clintons who died 'under other than natural circumstances'. The list was characterized by a US News and World Report article of the time as having 'serious deficiencies in corroborating evidence', and Congress declined to investigate the sitting president as being a serial murderer.

While the list was ignored by the mainstream media, it was embraced by the growing anti-Clinton conspiracy movement, stretching out to hundreds of names. Everyone from the elderly father of Hillary Clinton's physical therapist to the crew of a crashed military helicopter that Bill Clinton flew in once, were all said to have been liquidated by the Clintons in a never-ending purge dedicated to consolidating their power.

The list even became grist for the 2016 election, with Donald Trump calling the suicide of Vince Foster 'fishy'. The Foster conspiracy also came up during the contentious confirmation hearing of Supreme Court Justice Brett Kavanaugh. And yet none of the names on it have ever been proven to have been killed by the Clintons. What's more, many people who actually have been thorns in the side of the Clintons, such as the conspiracy theorists who have made millions off them, are still alive.

The congressman William Dannemeyer brought the idea of the Clinton Body Count into the mainstream.

WHY DOES ANYONE BELIEVE IT?

While theirs is the most famous, it's not just the Clintons who have a 'body count list' compiled in their name. Lists of suspicious deaths are common in conspiracy theory circles, with seemingly every powerful person and major event leaving behind a trail of mysterious suicides, crashes and murders.

Barack Obama has a death list with dozens of random names on it, including the health department official who released his birth certificate, Supreme Court Justice Antonin Scalia, a Hillary Clinton super delegate and a British banker. George W. Bush's body count list includes former Texas Air National Guard commanders, a conceptual artist and Commerce Secretary Ron Brown, who died in a plane crash – and is also on the Clintons' death lists. And there are voluminous lists of dead witnesses to the JFK assassination.

It's not implausible that powerful people like the Obamas or Clintons would have a huge number of professional and personal connections. Bill and Hillary Clinton both had thriving careers in law and politics before Bill made it to the White House in 1992. Statistically speaking, some of these people are going to pass away – most naturally of illness, but a few unnaturally or before their time. If one were to take every person Bill Clinton ever met or who worked under him who died, they'd make a long list indeed. But that doesn't mean the Clintons caused their deaths, or even had any particular connection to that person that would necessitate their death.

This is the biggest logical fallacy at the heart of such lists – they lack motive. Why would the Clintons want some random dentist or state trooper to die, but Monica Lewinsky and Donald Trump to live? Beyond that, these lists make every death seem unnatural, even simple old age or protracted illness. If it was an accident, they always play up how suspicious it was, and toss in that the findings of investigators were 'alleged' or 'apparent' – even if they were obvious. They play up unimportant details as the most important thing, such as the lack of an autopsy on a person who dies of cancer, or how many times a person Bill Clinton met once 30 years ago was shot. And when in doubt, they just lie. Say a person committed suicide via two shots (the most frequent claim about Vince Foster), or that

a plane 'exploded' when it crashed in bad weather. It doesn't matter.

These lists work not because they're accurate, but because they're long. They mistake quantity for veracity – a common trope in conspiracy circles that makes them easy to believe, and hard to debunk.

Ironically, the one name that would be a slam-dunk for such a Clinton Body Count list is almost always absent from the ones circulating on the internet. An enemy of the Clintons who relentlessly hounded them with conspiracy theories and unfounded accusations – original list creator Linda Thompson herself, who died in 2009 of a prescription drug overdose. If the Clintons didn't order Thompson to be killed, why believe they ordered anyone else to be killed?

CHAPTER 3

SECRET SOCIETIES

Throughout history, men – and women, but it is
predominantly men – have formed societies for the
mutual advancement of their members, to share
one another's proclivities, or simply to socialize with
like-minded individuals. That some of these societies
have been secretive cannot be denied. But just how
suspicious should we be of these mysterious groups
of people?

All Bilderberg meetings take place in impressive settings amidst tight security, such as this one in Dresden in 2009.

THE BILDERBERG GROUP

Take a small group of world leaders, sequester them in a luxury hotel surrounded by men with guns, keep their meetings shrouded in secrecy, and do it year after year. What do you end up with? A conspiracy theory about the elite getting together to talk about all of the horrible things they're going to do to the rest of us.

This is the crux of the Bilderberg Group, a small and ever-changing roster of notables in politics, business, academia and culture that meets yearly to discuss global issues. The group first met in 1954 at the Bilderberg Hotel in Oosterbeek, Holland to discuss the rise of anti-Americanism in Western Europe. It was comprised of one conservative and one liberal from each invited country, with the discussions informal, non-binding and, above all, secret. Since that first discussion, a steering committee has invited about 120 people to a different location for a weekend of conferences, held under Chatham House Rules, where any attendee of the meeting is free to use information from the discussion, but is not allowed to reveal who said it. As the leaked notes from one meeting put it, 'all participants spoke on an absolutely personal basis without committing any government or organization to which they might belong. In order to facilitate complete frankness, the discussions were confidential and no representatives of the press were admitted.'

While the actual discussions at Bilderberg Group meetings aren't disclosed, the list of attendees is. Among the luminaries to attend at least one Bilderberg meeting have been Bill Gates, Jeff Bezos, Angela Merkel, almost every modern British prime minister, Hillary and Bill Clinton, Henry Kissinger, multiple members of the Trump administration, Emanuel Macron, Prince Charles and countless other important and powerful people.

The leading conspiracy theorist Alex Jones gives a speech in July 2016. He has regularly denounced the Bilderberg Group.

Ex-US Secretary of State Henry Kissinger, former Vice President Nelson Rockefeller, and former President Gerald Ford in the White House. Henry Kissinger is one of many high-profile members of the Bilderberg Group.

Conspiracy theorists see the Bilderberg meetings as the most powerful people in the world talking about things they don't want anyone else to know about. The anti-Bilderberg faction has counted among its number Oklahoma City bomber Timothy McVeigh, 1999 London bomber David Copeland, Fidel Castro, conspiracy theory expert Alex Jones, American arch-conservatives and Osama Bin Laden. Those opposed to the Bilderberg Group describe conversation topics as nothing less than how to build a socialist uber-European government – or even worse, a one-world government devoted to crushing all opposition against it.

The popular conspiracy website Collective Evolution claims that Bilderberg is made up of 'a small group of people and the corporations they run [who] completely control all aspects of human life', and charts out the links between Bilderberg participants and pretty much everything else imaginable. Another highly viewed conspiracy site, GlobalResearch.ca, cites a 'Bilderberg wish list', including 'centralized control of world populations by "mind control"', 'a New World Order with no middle class, only rulers and servants', 'a zero-growth society without prosperity or progress, only greater wealth and power for the rulers', and a 'global welfare state where obedient slaves will be rewarded and non-conformists targeted for extermination'.

The Bilderberg Group meetings are also lumped in with other conspiracy theorist touchstones like the Illuminati, Skull and Bones Society, Trilateral Commission, the Freemasons, the New World Order and the Council on Foreign Relations. While their relationships to each other are a Venn diagram of accusations, at heart, they're all believed to desire a cashless society ruled by mass socialism, culled with genocide or eugenics, and where our rights are taken away in exchange for security from threats they've created. There are long lists of quotes from prominent Bilderberg attendees, such as Bill Gates appearing to claim he wants to use vaccines to cull the population, to Henry Kissinger spouting off about aliens landing on Earth.

And all of this is done without any accountability to the people or access to the press, in luxury hotels surrounded by armed guards, razor wire and even helicopters. As David Rockefeller was reported to have said at the 1991 Bilderberg meeting, 'It would have been impossible for us to develop our plan for the world if we had been subjected to the lights of publicity during those years.' Enterprising journalists are constantly prevented from reporting on meetings, with heavy security harassing reporters who try to get close, and a few long-time Bilderberg chroniclers even being arrested. As the theory goes, if Bilderberg members were not conspiring to do us harm, then they wouldn't meet in secret. Only people with something to hide feel like they have to hide what they're doing.

BANAL MEETINGS OF IMPORTANT PEOPLE

There's little separating the conspiracy theories about the Bilderberg Group from those about any other

of who will be destroyed next, the topics are aggressively normal, even banal. For example, the notes of the 1958 meeting in Turkey contain discussions about how the West regards China, the future of NATO, increasing cooperation with the US, and early notes on economic unification in Europe. The meeting in Cannes in 1963 had discussions about the recently concluded Cuban Missile Crisis, France's rejection of the UK joining the European Economic Community, criticism of outsized American military spending, and fostering trade with the developing world. And the 1980 meeting notes, from Aachen, Germany, contain frank talk about the alliance between the United States and Western Europe, observations about Iran, ruminations on the SALT

The Taschenbergpalais Hotel in Dresden served as the 2016 meeting place for the annual conference of the shadowy Bilderberg Group.

nuclear arms treaty, whether or not European nations should join the American boycott of the 1980 Moscow Olympics, and how NATO should regard future Russian aggression.

The discussions are frank and not always complimentary, but are able to take place because the speakers know they'll be kept anonymous. In keeping with Chatham House Rules, points made during discussions are written out in detail, but given little or no attribution. Commenters are referred to as 'a Portuguese speaker', or 'a French participant belonging to the government majority group', or simply 'one participant'. Nobody is making any decisions, giving any orders, or putting their country in an untenable position. There are certainly no references to total domination, mass killing, world government, or anything else conspiratorial. The need for secrecy goes hand in hand with the nature of the meetings, and any large enough gathering of powerful people is going to have outsized security.

Despite the protests, intrigue, conspiracy theories and secrecy, the Bilderberg Group is an important tool for fostering international relations and finding new solutions to difficult problems. And if it were used for anything truly horrible, its members probably wouldn't be so open about it.

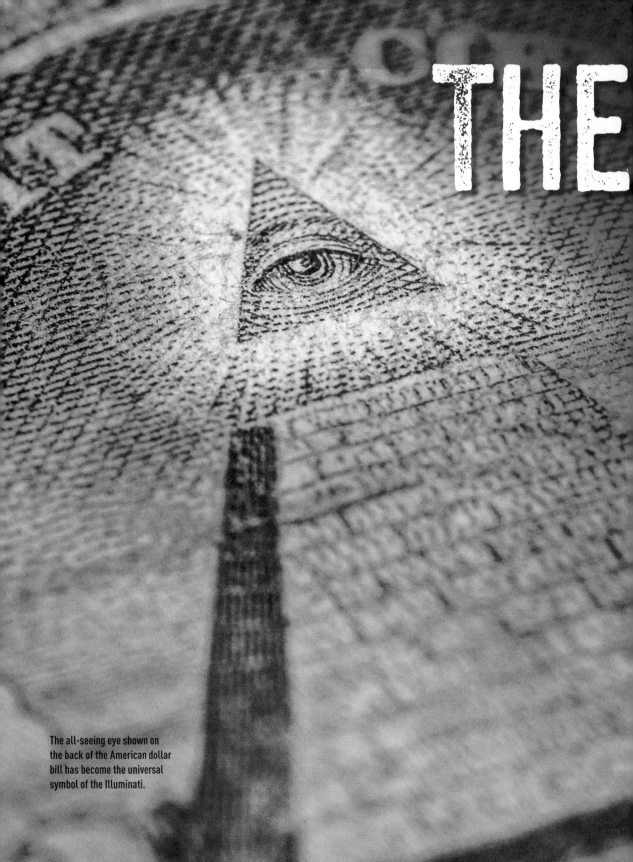

THE

The all-seeing eye shown on the back of the American dollar bill has become the universal symbol of the Illuminati.

ILLUMINATI

Conspiracy theorists obsess about ancient, world-controlling secret societies, full of rich and powerful titans, pulling the strings on the rest of us. And there might be no secret society more ancient, more powerful and more controlling than the Illuminati. Paradoxically, it's also the most famous, least impactful and, ultimately, most misunderstood of all the supposed secret societies. Like many other conspiracy theories, there is a grain of truth to some of these accusations, in that there was a historical Illuminati. And it was crushed just as its power was beginning to grow. But it has no relation to the modern conception of the Illuminati – only to old stereotypes and fears of the unknown.

THE OLD NEW WORLD ORDER

According to over two centuries of accusations, made in everything from self-published pamphlets to Twitter, the Illuminati is the centuries-old cabal that controls every aspect of our politics, finance, culture, entertainment and economics. Its bloodlines include generations of world leaders, religious icons, titans of industry and bankers; as well as an ever-growing

The Illuminati are seen as puppet masters, determining the course of world history.

The French Revolution, along with many other major historical events, has been attributed to the machinations of the Illuminati.

roster of musicians, actors, sports figures and internet celebrities, many of whom are merely pawns of the Illuminati, mind-controlled to espouse its beliefs to the uneducated masses.

And if something nefarious happens somewhere in the world, it's a good bet that the Illuminati made it happen, for a reason only known to them. Assassinations, currency manipulation, wars staged to sell arms to both sides, foreign coups, empires rising and falling, and even man-made disasters? All in the playbook of the Illuminati.

None of this happens in a vacuum. Pattern-seeking is an essential element of human thought, looking for ways to predict when the next predator will jump out of the bushes, or trying to figure out that if we don't feed and water our crops, we die. People desperately

need to believe that things happen for a reason, that there's meaning in the events of our lives, and not just random events cascading on top of each other. We need someone or something to be in control. And for a long time, that was the Illuminati.

So what are the Illuminati said to control? Virtually every major event of the last few centuries, starting with the French Revolution, moving through the Napoleonic and World Wars, peaking with the Kennedy assassination, and continuing through the 11 September attacks. They keep an iron grip on politics, starting wars to get their way. Or as one popular conspiracy book, *Bloodlines of the Illuminati* puts it, once you are awake to the Illuminati, 'wars between kings no longer appear as wars between elite factions, but contrived wars to control the masses by their greedy elite masters'.

Naturally, they jealously guard their wealth and power, killing anyone who opposes them, rigging economies to ensure their empires expand, and inserting secret brainwashing messages into entertainment and literature to stealthily let us know that they are in control. Every major world politician and titan of industry has a blood relationship to the Illuminati, from the Rockefellers to the Roosevelts to the Rothschilds.

Not only does the Illuminati have its hooks into virtually every aspect of our society, they're allied with the Freemasons, another shadowy cabal full of secrets and symbols. They've got links to the New World Order, the supposed one-world government conspiracy theory of the 1990s. They reinforce their hold over us by putting symbols on our money (the 'all seeing eye' on the US dollar bill), monitor us through the National Security Agency, control our weather, health and food; and send out an endless roster of celebrities to dazzle our unthinking minds with displays of loyalty and human sacrifice.

As Alex Jones has said of the Illuminati, the shadowy group is no less than 'an intergalactic invasion into this space through people. I'm telling you, it's what all the ancients said. It's what they warned of. It's what we're dealing with. They're demons! They're frickin' interdimensional invaders, OK?'

'THE HIGHEST POSSIBLE DEGREE OF MORALITY'

The real, historical Illuminati movement was founded on 1 May 1776 in Bavaria, by Adam Weishaupt, a professor of Canon Law at the University of Ingolstadt. He was also an ardent foe of the doctrinal and conservative Catholicism of the Jesuits who ran the college.

A liberal secularist, he rankled at the influence of Catholic doctrine over philosophy and the sciences, as well as its control of the Bavarian monarchy. Weishaupt and those who agreed with him went underground, and after being rejected by the Freemasons, they formed their own secret society, borrowing some of the Freemasons' rank system and terminology, but with a far more liberal ideology – one devoted to equality, the embrace of new ideas and fighting the abuses of a corrupt state and the dogma of a controlling Church.

It took two years for the group to settle on the name 'Order of Illuminati', selecting for its logo the Owl of Minerva, the Greek symbol of wisdom. In those early years, it measured its membership in single digits,

Adam Weishaupt, the eighteenth-century political and religious radical who founded the society known as the Illuminati.

The Owl of Minerva, depicted on an Ancient Greek coin.

and only about 650 men ever obtained even one of the three degrees Weishaupt's society offered (the Freemasons have 33 degrees). By the early 1780s, it was still just a debating society, as Weishaupt and a few acolytes espoused anti-religious and pro-equality ideas to a few dozen ardent believers. They also poached members of other Masonic lodges, and while they later claimed to have about 2,500 members in total, it was probably far smaller.

By 1785, the group had found a few powerful benefactors, and was expanding into other cities and universities. Alarmed by the expansion of these anti-state, anti-Church teachings, and driven by the general anti-secularism of the times, Duke of Bavaria Charles Theodore banned all secret societies, sending infiltrators in to root them out. The duke's tightening net sent Weishaupt fleeing, ending the group after less than ten years.

It wasn't until decades later that several popular conspiracy theory books became the foundation for an argument that the Illuminati not only hadn't been broken by Charles Theodore but was far more powerful than anyone imagined. These books were particularly embraced by anti-Masonic conspiracy theorists, and blamed their ideas for the carnage of the French Revolution – a movement which shared many philosophical traits, but had an entirely different method of accomplishing them.

Those books offered no real evidence that the original Illuminati society even had goals of world domination and enslavement of the masses. In fact, Weishaupt saw the society's goal as 'to attain the highest possible degree of morality and virtue, and to lay the foundation for the reformation of the world by the association of good men to oppose the progress of moral evil'. As Thomas Jefferson wrote in 1800, 'Wishaupt [sic] believes that to promote this perfection of the human character was the object of Jesus Christ. That his intention was simply to reinstate natural religion, & by diffusing the light of his morality, to teach us to govern ourselves.'

Neither of these quotes sound like the modern perception of the Illuminati as a war-starting, string-pulling cabal. They sound much more like historical perceptions of the Jewish people, who were tagged with many of the same conspiracy theories that the Illuminati had applied to them. Nonetheless, the Illuminati became the fodder for countless conspiracy theories, books, games and internet memes.

Weishaupt's society was intellectual, egalitarian and moralistic. It was also small, young and had little influence in Bavarian society. And once that started to change, it was crushed. Whatever other secrets it held were made public at the time. There's no real evidence that any parallel or subsequent Illuminati has had any influence on any events since.

Charles Theodore, the Duke of Bavaria from 1777–99, banned all secret societies in his territory, including the Illuminati.

GOD'S BANKER:

Roberto Calvi in a Milan Courtroom 1981, after spending three years on the run. Calvi was sentenced to four years in prison for fraud, but was released on bail to await an appeal.

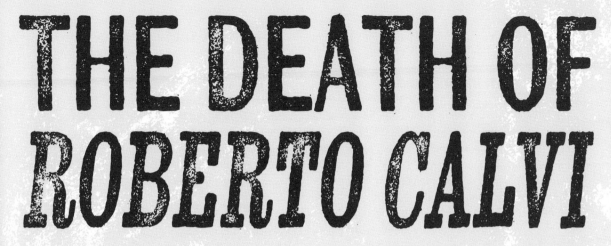

THE DEATH OF ROBERTO CALVI

The death of Roberto Calvi, nicknamed 'God's banker' because of his close links with the Vatican, shocked the world in 1982, when he was found hanging beneath Blackfriars Bridge in London. Initially, his death was seen as suicide, but it soon emerged that murder was a much more likely scenario. Disturbing evidence came to light when the case was investigated, for it appeared that Calvi's shady financial dealings not only involved Italy's largest private bank and a secret Italian Masonic organization but the Vatican itself. To this day, the complex plot involving the bank, the Freemasons and the Vatican continues to unravel and it is still unclear exactly what happened. However, there seems to be no doubt that the Vatican was politically and financially implicated in the scandal, whether directly or indirectly.

SHADY DEALINGS

At the time of his death, 62-year-old Calvi was a successful businessman, the chairman of Banco Ambrosiana in Milan. Over his career he had built the bank up from a small concern to a large international organization with a huge financial empire. However, in 1978 Banco Ambrosiana was investigated by the Bank of Italy and found to be guilty of illegally exporting billions of lire. Calvi went on the run, and the bank began to collapse. Three years later, he was arrested, tried and sentenced to four years in prison. After a short period of detention he was released on bail pending an appeal, but he had other charges to answer as well. At the time of his murder he was also being investigated for making fraudulent deals in the United States with a Sicilian banker called Michele Sindona.

As the investigations continued it emerged that the Vatican had a shareholding in Banco Ambrosiana and that Calvi was closely linked to Archbishop Paul Marcinkus, the head of the Vatican Bank. Enormous sums of money had been siphoned off from Banco Ambrosiana into the so-called 'Institute for Religious Works', headed by Marcinkus, and there was speculation that this money had gone to fund right-wing regimes in Latin America that were friendly to the United States government and the Vatican. Another player in this complex game was Licio Gelli, a former Nazi, who ran a Masonic lodge known as Propaganda Due, or P2. This secret organization had a membership of over 1,000 prominent politicians, businessmen and criminals, who were all united in a spirit of anti-communism as well as being dedicated to the enhancement of their own personal wealth and power.

MURDER NOT SUICIDE

In 1998 Calvi's family caused his body to be exhumed and, four years later, the initial verdict of suicide was overturned. It transpired that Calvi had been found with five bricks in his pocket and his hands tied behind his back. Moreover, his neck showed no signs of damage and there were none of his own fingerprints on the bricks. All of this pointed to the fact that he had not committed suicide as a reaction to financial ruination, but had been cold-bloodedly murdered by his enemies in the world of high finance and organized crime.

The killing had all the hallmarks of a Mafia-style execution. Police in Rome and London began to track down several suspects. Pippo Calo, a prominent member of the Sicilian Mafia; Flavio Carboni, a businessman with many interests all over the world; Carboni's ex-girlfriend, Manuela Kleinzig; Ernesto Diotallevi, the leader of a criminal organization in Rome called the 'Banda della Magliana'; and a Mafia financier named

Francesco Di Carlo. On 18 April 2005, the City of London police force charged Calo, Carboni, Kleinzig and Diotallevi with the murder.

AN UNHOLY MOB

In recent years, it has been suggested that the real reason that Calvi was murdered was to prevent him from making known the links between the Vatican, the P2 Freemasons and the Mafia. During his time at Banco Ambrosiana, enormous sums of money were transferred into the Vatican's coffers, resulting in the ultimate bankruptcy of Ambrosiana and its shareholders. (The day before Calvi died, his secretary Teresa Corrocher committed suicide by jumping out of a high window at the bank's headquarters. She left a note blaming her boss.)

It seems that Calvi and Gelli were in league. Calvi had been passing money from Ambrosiano and the Vatican Bank to Gelli and others, who in turn were busy negotiating political deals such as the sale of the Exocet missile from France to Argentina. In the view of many critics, the Vatican acted as a country with right-wing political interests, bankrolling whatever initiatives seemed beneficial to the Pope and the Catholic Church, whether in Latin America or Europe. This was done secretly, with no regard whatsoever to democratic or sovereign rights in those countries. Obviously, if any of this information came out, it would be highly damaging to the Pope and the Vatican, who liked to preserve an image of being above politics.

THE DEATH OF JOHN PAUL I

When John Paul I took office as Pope in 1978, it looked as though some of the activities of Archbishop Marcinkus and the 'Institute for Religious Works' would have to come to an end. However, John Paul I died only 33 days after his election, apparently of a

The death of Calvi raised questions about the role of the Vatican in politics and its susceptibility to corruption.

heart attack. Some suspected foul play and indeed there were a number of anomalies surrounding the death, which was not well handled by the Vatican health carers. The Vatican press office also made many errors in reporting the death. In keeping with Vatican law, no post-mortem was performed on the Pope, which also caused some commentators to question what had happened. A controversy ensued, with some claiming that the Pope had been murdered and others holding the opposite view. For example, in his book, *In God's Name*, David Yallop suggested that the Pope had been in danger the moment he took office. John Cornwell rejected this theory in his own book, *A Thief in the Night*, claiming that the Pope died as the result of a pulmonary embolism. He further suggested that the Vatican had acted in an incompetent, rather than a criminal, manner both during and after the tragedy. Whatever the truth of the matter, it seems that in terms of its political and financial dealings in the 1970s and 1980s, the Vatican had a great deal to hide. To this day, we still do not know the full extent of its involvement in the Calvi affair. Perhaps the ongoing trial will finally reveal the truth.

Licio Gelli, the leader of Propaganda Due, had shady links to Calvi.

John-Paul I lying in state after he passed away in 1979, just 33 days after becoming Pope.

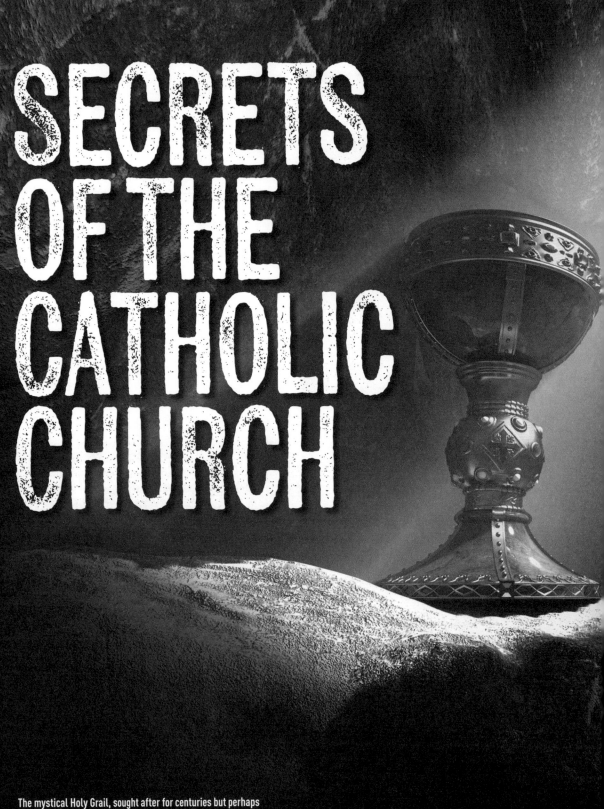

SECRETS OF THE CATHOLIC CHURCH

The mystical Holy Grail, sought after for centuries but perhaps
just a metaphor for the bloodline of Jesus

THE KNIGHTS TEMPLAR

The Christian Church has been a natural target for conspiracy theorists throughout almost the whole of its existence. In centuries past, these theorists would have been called heretics and burnt at the stake. In these more enlightened days they post their ideas on the internet and write bestselling novels.

Two subjects that appeal to conspiracy theorists are the Knights Templar and the Holy Grail. The Knights Templar were an order of warrior monks based in Jerusalem during the time of the Crusades. They were believed to be fabulously wealthy and they became so powerful that in 1307 Philip IV of France led a campaign against them. Members of the order were arrested and tortured until they confessed to heresy. Their influence lingered on for many years, especially in Portugal and Scotland, but they gradually disappeared from view. However, many theorists believe that the order actually went underground instead of dying out and that it is still in existence.

Members of the military order of the Templars. The order was persecuted for heresy and then disbanded by the French King Philip IV in 1307, but the conspiracy theories surrounding it have not gone away.

THE HOLY GRAIL

Even more mysterious than the Knights Templar is the Holy Grail, one of the great myths of Christianity. The Holy Grail was supposedly the cup that caught the blood of Jesus during his crucifixion. The story goes that the cup was kept by a friend of Jesus, Joseph of Arimathea, who might have taken it to France, or perhaps even Glastonbury in England. Some believe that it was taken to Jerusalem in the Holy Land: others claim that it has been kept in Genoa, Valencia or Rosslyn Chapel in Scotland. According to some accounts, it might even have fallen into the hands of the Knights Templar. Wherever it landed up, it became a mythical object over time and it was credited with extraordinary magical powers.

The risen Christ appears to Mary Magdalene in Veronese's painting *Noli Me Tangere*. But was Christ ever actually dead?

Stories have circulated about the Holy Grail and the Knights Templar for centuries, but a modern bestseller *Holy Blood, Holy Grail*, published in 1982, suggested that behind these mysteries lay an even greater one – one that went to the very heart of the Christian faith. According to the authors of the book, the Holy Grail was not a cup at all: that was the result of a mistake in translation. The real Christian treasure was not the Holy Grail but the Holy Blood. That is, the true secret was not the existence of a mere cup but of a bloodline of the descendants of Jesus.

THE MAGDALENE CONSPIRACY

According to this theory, Jesus had two children, the products of a clandestine marriage to Mary Magdalene. These children, so the story goes, were brought to France by Mary Magdalene and Joseph of Arimathea. The oldest child died but the second son went on to have children whose descendants would become the (real) Merovingian Kings of France between the fifth and eighth centuries AD. After the Merovingian Kings were overthrown, their legacy was protected by the Knights Templar and their great secret – together with the evidence to back it up – was hidden away. Its existence was only hinted at by obscure codes.

With the end of the Knights Templar, so this theory goes, all evidence of the bloodline of Jesus disappeared from view for over 500 years. It was only in 1885 that someone began to penetrate the mystery, a young priest named François Bérenger Saunière, who was assigned to the parish at Rennes-le-Chateau, an ancient walled town in the French Pyrenees.

Plantard examined the mysteries of Rennes-le-Chateau and used what he found there to bolster his questionable genealogical claims that he was descended from the Merovingian Kings.

Saunière began to restore the town's sixth-century church. As he did so, he found a series of parchments hidden inside a hollow pillar. These parchments included some genealogical information and a collection of ciphers and codes. Allegedly the secrets of these codes made Saunière a wealthy man and he later spent much of his money on commissioning strange new artefacts for the church.

THE PRIORY OF SION

With Saunière's death the trail once again went cold, only to be revived by a Frenchman named Pierre Plantard who wrote extensively about the mysteries of Rennes-le-Chateau. He claimed that knowledge of the descendants of Jesus had remained in the hands of a mysterious organization called the Priory of Sion,

an ancient secret order that lay behind the Knights Templar and guarded their legacy. Notable members included Leonardo da Vinci and Isaac Newton.

Sadly, this exotic theory convinced few historians, many of whom were amused to discover that Pierre Plantard had registered the Priory of Sion as his own organization. He had also transparently forged genealogical documents, allegedly discovered by Saunière, which appeared to demonstrate that Plantard himself was a direct descendant of the Merovingian Kings – and thus of Jesus Christ himself!

And if all that sounds like the stuff of bestselling fiction rather than history, author Dan Brown can only agree with you. This most entertaining but unlikely of conspiracy theories formed the basis of his global bestseller, *The Da Vinci Code*.

THE PROTOCOLS OF THE ELDERS OF ZION

The document known as *The Protocols of the Elders of Zion* is one of the earliest, most successful and enduring of all conspiracy theories. First circulated in Russia during the early twentieth century, it purports to be a kind of manual for world domination that was written by a mysterious cabal of Jewish elders. It was then used to fuel fears that there was an international Jewish conspiracy that sought to take over the world. So successful was it in its aims that it has been used again and again over the ensuing century. Wherever there has been a rush of anti-Semitism, from Hitler's Germany to the training camps of Al-Qaeda, you can guarantee that a copy of *The Protocols of the Elders of Zion* will never be hard to find.

The document may only have appeared in its currently recognized form in the final years of Tsarist Russia, but it has its roots in the mid-nineteenth century. The story begins with a French popular novel called *The Mysteries of the People*, written by Eugène Sue, which featured a group of Jesuits that were plotting to take over the world. This notion of a massive conspiracy was then taken up by the French satirist Maurice Joly, who used it in an 1864 pamphlet titled 'Dialogues in Hell Between Machiavelli and Montesquieu', which attacked the political ambitions of the then French ruler, Napoleon III. This time, however, the plotters, as the title suggests, were operating from beyond the grave.

Then, in 1868, Hermann Goedsche, a German anti-Semite and spy, wrote a book named *Biarritz*. This included a chapter entitled 'The Jewish Cemetery in Prague and the Council of Representatives of the Twelve Tribes of Israel'. The chapter described an imaginary secret rabbinical cabal meeting which was held in the cemetery at midnight every hundred years to plan the agenda for the Jewish Conspiracy. The set-up was plainly taken from an Alexandre Dumas novel, while the supposed secret agenda was actually straight from Joly's 'Dialogues in Hell...'

SECRET POLICE

However, turning the supposed conspirators from Jesuits or dead philosophers into Jews touched a nerve and by the 1890s copies of this chapter of Goedsche's book, now treated as fact rather than fantasy or satire, were starting to circulate in Russia. Before long the Tsar's secret police, the Okhrana, recognized the potential popularity of the material and one of their operatives, Matvei Golovinski, worked up a book-length version of this fantastical Zionist plot. The book, now known as *The Protocols of the Elders of Zion*, was widely circulated and was undoubtedly influential in inflaming the anti-Jewish pogrom that swept Russia in 1905–06.

Vladimir Lenin preaches to the masses, Russia 1917. The fact that some Bolshevik leaders were Jewish was taken by many as proof of the worldwide Jewish conspiracy.

Curiously, one of the visions put forward by the Protocols – that of a small group taking over a huge country – was repeated by the real events of a decade later when the 1917 Bolshevik Revolution transformed Russia. Before long this was seen by many as evidence that the Bolshevik Revolution was in fact part of the Jewish conspiracy. Jews and communists were now bracketed together across much of the world and the Protocols were put forward as damning evidence.

Henry Ford sponsored the printing of half a million copies of *The Protocols of the Elders of Zion* in the United States.

The Protocols were popular with right-wing elements in 1920s Germany and also in the United States. No less a man than Henry Ford sponsored the printing of half a million copies in America.

Then the debunking began in earnest. Experts looked at the document and soon noticed that its origins lay in pulp fiction rather than historical fact. In 1920, one Lucien Wolf published an exposé tracing the history of the Protocols back to the works of Goedsche and Joly.

The Times soon followed suit and, later that year, a book documenting the hoax was published in the United States by Herman Bernstein.

ADOLF HITLER

One might have thought that this would have been the end of the tale. Sadly not. By the 1920s anti-Semitism was endemic, nowhere more so than in Germany. Adolf Hitler referred to the Protocols in *Mein Kampf*: 'To what extent the whole existence of this people is based on a continuous lie is shown incomparably by the Protocols of the Wise Men of Zion, so infinitely hated by the Jews', he wrote. He acknowledged the claims that the book was a forgery but ignored them, claiming instead that 'with positively terrifying certainty they reveal the nature and activity of the Jewish people and expose their inner contexts as well as their ultimate final aims'.

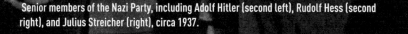

Senior members of the Nazi Party, including Adolf Hitler (second left), Rudolf Hess (second right), and Julius Streicher (right), circa 1937.

Once the Nazis took power in Germany the book became a set text in schools and helped fuel all the horrors of the Holocaust. It did not matter to the German Nazis that in 1934 a Swiss Nazi was brought to court after he had published a series of articles accepting the Protocols as fact. The trial, known as the Berne Trial, finished in May 1935 when the court declared the Protocols to be forgeries, plagiarisms and obscene literature. As far as Hitler was concerned, however, a lurid lie beat the truth every time and the Swiss verdict was completely ignored.

The palpable falsity of the Protocols has not stopped their circulation in more recent times, either. They are widely published across the Arab world and have proved particularly popular in Iran, Egypt and Saudi Arabia, where they have been used to inflame opinion over the whole Palestinian question. In America, too, the Protocols are still accepted as fact by both neo-Nazi organizations and Louis Farrakhan's Nation of Islam, which has distributed copies.

The history of the Protocols demonstrates that a powerful conspiracy theory need not have any factual basis to gain acceptance: it also reminds us that false conspiracy theories can do an enormous amount of harm if they are cynically used to back up the worst political objectives and to persecute innocent people.

THE GEMSTONE FILES

One of the most outrageous and entertaining global conspiracy theories is that of the mysterious Gemstone Files. This theory in essence suggests that the Mafia, led for a time by Aristotle Onassis, controlled America during the 1950s and 1960s.

Allegedly, the original Gemstone Files were compiled from a series of writings and talks given by a man named Bruce Roberts in San Francisco during the late sixties and early seventies. The mysterious Roberts was supposedly responsible for inventing the synthetic ruby used in laser technology, but claimed to have been swindled out of his discovery by the Howard Hughes organization. He also claimed to have been involved in, or have knowledge of, a whole range of intelligence operations. He frequented a San Francisco pub called the Drift Inn where he would entertain his fellow regulars – including ex-intelligence agents – with improbable stories of outlandish secrets. Some of these may have been recorded and transcribed by the pub landlord. Others were written down by Roberts himself. Collected together, they run to over a thousand pages.

It's hard to know for sure, though, as very few, if any people, have ever seen the original manuscript. Instead what people have read is something called the Skeleton Key to the Gemstone File, a 30-page summary of the original produced by one Stephanie Caruana, who was introduced to the original by a conspiracy theorist called Mae Brussell. All of this is hard to check because the mysterious Roberts allegedly died of cancer in 1975, and Mae Brussell died in 1988. As for the original files, according to another conspiracy theorist named

According to the Gemstone Files conspiracy theory, Aristotle Onassis, a Mafia leader, actually ran the United States for nearly two decades in the 1950s and 1960s.

The Gemstone Files proposed sordid connections between the Mafia, the CIA and the FBI and claimed that they were responsible for some of the most high-profile assassinations of the 20th century.

Bill Keith, who has written a book about them, there are only four or five photocopies in existence and the owners refuse to part with them.

ONASSIS THE MAFIA BOSS!

So what we are left with is Caruana's Skeleton Key. This document was first hinted at in an article Caruana wrote for Playgirl magazine (of all the unlikely places for a sensational journalistic exposé). Then, in 1974, she began to circulate photocopies of the Skeleton Key itself. These were copied and re-copied by conspiracy enthusiasts around the world. Partly because most copies looked illicit, the document soon gained an underground reputation.

So what was in the Gemstone Files, according to this Skeleton Key? Essentially, it is an impressionistic alternative history of the post-war era, one that weaves links between the CIA, FBI, and the Mafia, and seeks to explain the deaths of JFK, LBJ and Martin Luther King. Along the way, it brings in Ted Kennedy, Richard Nixon and San Francisco's Mayor Joe Alioto. At the heart of the conspiracy are two shadowy figures, Howard Hughes and Aristotle Onassis.

According to the Gemstone Files, Onassis was a drug dealer who made his fortune selling opium to Turkey before going into partnership with Joe Kennedy (JFK's father) to smuggle booze into the USA during Prohibition. By the 1950s, Onassis was running the Mafia. Meanwhile, the Texan millionaire Howard Hughes was buying up politicians with a view to controlling the presidency. Onassis saw Hughes as a rival, kidnapped him and replaced him with a double (which explains why Hughes became a recluse in his later years). Now Onassis controlled both the Mafia and a number of key politicians. In the 1960 election both candidates, Kennedy and Nixon, were beholden to him – so either way, he won.

However, when Kennedy pulled back from invading Cuba, the Mafia decided to have him killed. And so on, and so on. Every assassination during the sixties could be laid at the feet of this sinister conspiracy. Particularly bizarre are the allegations that Onassis kept the real Howard Hughes prisoner on his private Greek island and only married Jackie Kennedy as part of his revenge on the treacherous JFK.

FROM GEMSTONES TO X-FILES

All in all, Onassis emerges more as a Bond super-villain than a real person. And that may be the key to the Gemstone Files' enduring popularity. This is the Bond movie version of modern history – more colourful and exciting than real life could ever be. And, in turn, the kind of conspiracy theories propounded in the Gemstone Files have definitely influenced many movies: the notions inform Oliver Stone's films like *JFK* and *Nixon*, and have also influenced TV shows like the *X-Files*.

So do the Gemstone Files have any serious credibility at all? Well, some of the many theories that are bandied about in their pages do bear consideration. That there was some kind of connection between JFK and the Mafia, for instance, seems certain. Overall though, the Files are clearly written by someone who had a few nuggets of inside knowledge, but proceeded to put two and two together and make a million. As for whether the real author was the mysterious Roberts, or whether Brussell or Caruana was actually the author of the Files, remains open to speculation. Whoever the author was, though, the Gemstone Files are ultimately an entertaining and remarkably influential work of fiction.

Texan millionaire Howard Hughes made his fortune from the film and aviation industries.

THE REPTILE

Reptoid. Reptilian. Draconian. Saurian. Lizard men. Anunnaki. Lizard aliens. The Reptile Elite. While they go by many names, all describe reptile-like aliens from a faraway star that have infiltrated Earth's governments, taking human form to manipulate events on the planet. By taking human beings and harvesting us for scientific information (through devouring our flesh and blood, naturally), the reptilians have wormed their way into our society, taking control of our nations, paving the way for their eventual invasion – and our conquest.

Reptile-like aliens are a stock trope of both conspiracy theories and science fiction, usually given shape-shifting and mind controlling powers, and almost always bent on doing evil to humans. But they're also a huge part of ancient mythology, literature, folklore, pseudo-history and even video gaming. Many different cultures have depicted winged serpents, man-snakes and lizard people as part of their creation myths. With so many depictions of reptile aliens, and so many deeds ascribed to them, it can be difficult to keep track of what is an actual, legitimate legend about leathery visitors from the sky, and what's just the bizarre opinion of a fringe author.

So are reptoids real? Are they walking among us, wearing the skin of Queen Elizabeth, Barack Obama, Warren Buffett, Hillary Clinton and other leaders? Do they have underground bases around the United States? Are they waging a war with other, equally powerful aliens? And have they been planning their conquest for thousands of years?

TWELVE-FOOT TALL, BLOOD-DRINKING SHAPE-SHIFTERS – OR NOT

The longer a conspiracy theory sticks around, the more irrelevant details it picks up. So any dive into the mythology around the reptilian alien theory becomes

ELITE

bogged down in fake alien hierarchies, biology, geology and history. Some of it intertwines with ours, some of it spirals off into digressions about angels, gods and vast intergalactic empires. The deeper one goes, the more it all seems like a mash-up of Star Trek, the Bible and heavily trod UFO mythology. But little of it was simply made up on the spot. Reptilian humanoids have been part of pop culture for nearly a century, making one of their first literary appearances in the fiction of *Conan the Barbarian* creator Robert E. Howard in the late 1920s. But it was prolific conspiracy theorist David Icke who

first cemented the idea of a powerful Reptilian Elite pulling the strings on the human race in his 1998 book *The Biggest Secret: The Book That Will Change the World*.

The basics of Icke's 'biggest secret' are that reptile aliens from the star Sigma Draconis (18.8 light years from Earth) came to our world in ancient times. Seeing the planet as an opportunity for plunder, they used their shape-shifting abilities to interbreed with humans, spawning dozens of royal bloodlines, and quickly becoming our rulers. They now make up virtually every royal dynasty, most wealthy families, legendary cultural

Are there secretly reptilian aliens hiding beneath the faces of some of the world's most powerful people? That is what some conspiracy theorists would have you believe.

figures, bankers, great scientists and nearly three dozen presidents. They are said to control unimaginable wealth, power and military might. And they manipulate all of it in the service of fighting their own war, against the beings colloquially known as the 'grey aliens' – a race of diminutive, large-eyed humanoids from Zeta Reticuli, located about 39 light years from Earth.

Icke's reptilians were the culmination of years of his exploration of new age spirituality, alternative medicine, ancient legends, Christian eschatology and prophecy. They were also derided as fascist, anti-Semitic and completely insane. And they skyrocketed in popularity as Icke wrote about them more, and further developed his mythology. Books like *Children of the Matrix*, *The David Icke Guide to the Global Conspiracy: And How to End It* and *Human Race Get Off Your Knees*, spilled out more details about the lizard-human hybrids that control our world, exactly what they'd done to us, and how we had to free ourselves from their clawed grip.

'They're feeding off humanity,' Icke told Vice in 2012. 'They're turning humanity into a slave race. They demand human sacrifice – that's where Satanism comes in. They feed off human energy. They feed off the energy of children.' Other conspiracy theorists ran with the concept, and soon there was an ecosystem of websites and books about the horrid doings of the lizard people, and about their war with the grey aliens. One site posits that the Hall of the Pontifical Audiences, where the Pope has held large gatherings since the early 1970s, is shaped like a snake's head; while other conspiracy sites add incomprehensible details to the grey/reptoid war, even positing a peace treaty between the greys and the United States. A video on the YouTube channel 'Reptilian Resistance' got over 3.2 million views showing how a Secret Service agent protecting Barack Obama is actually a lizard alien. Icke counts *The Color*

David Icke is the most well-known advocate of the reptilian conspiracy theory.

The Hall of Pontifical Audiences in Rome is shaped like a snake's head, supposedly providing evidence of the conspiracy.

Purple author Alice Walker and mainstream right-wing media figures as admirers of his. And Icke himself has sold over half a million books in just the United States and England.

It's clear that despite its outlandishness, the Reptilian Elite conspiracy theory has caught on with at least some segment of the population. But what is it that they really believe?

'NOT A JEWISH PLOT'

Icke's reptilian elite conspiracy theory feels novel, but it's a mishmash of UFO abduction stories, urban legends, pop tropes and old conspiracy theories. There's little in Icke's books that can't be gleaned from other sources. Lizard-like beings populate the mythology of ancient Greece, Rome, China and Egypt. There are stories as far back as the 1930s of lizard people being on our Earth and digging vast tunnels, along with more modern pop

Lizard-men commonly featured in mythology. Sobek, an ancient Egyptian god with a crocodile head, is one such example.

depictions of reptoids, like a 1973 episode of *Doctor Who* featuring lizard aliens called Draconians, the mini-series V (which has almost the same plot of lizards in human disguises) and the lizard-like Gorn alien from the *Star Trek* episode 'Arena'.

Likewise, much of the mythology around the grey aliens, supposedly the sworn enemies of the reptilians, is pulled from alien abduction stories like that of Betty and Barney Hill from 1961, or the legends about the 1947 Roswell crash. And the 'bloodlines' element of the reptilians comes straight from mythology about the Illuminati. Icke even conflates the two at times, and the supposed membership and dirty deeds of the two are basically the same.

There's another aspect to the Reptile Elite conspiracy theory that can't be ignored: anti-Semitism. Icke claims not to be anti-Semitic, and has said that the reptoid conspiracy 'is not a plot on the world by Jewish people'. But his descriptions of the lizard elite as shape-shifting, blood-drinking and dedicated to conniving evil match up with classically racist descriptions of Jews. He has embraced Holocaust denial, calling *Schindler's List* tyrannical indoctrination that shows 'the unchallenged version of events'. And in his book *The Truth Shall Set You Free*, Icke lays out exactly who is to blame for all the world's woes, writing, 'I strongly believe that a small Jewish clique which has contempt for the mass of Jewish people worked with non-Jews to create World War I, the Russian Revolution and the Second World War.'

The anti-Jewish sentiment that undergirds the Reptile Elite is common to conspiracy theories, where Jews are blamed for everything from supposed genocide to the flat Earth movement. Icke didn't make it up, he merely found a new way to monetize it. Ultimately, his conspiracy theory isn't especially novel or unique, only compelling to people who want to find an alien explanation for human events that they don't like.

THE ROTHSCHILD BANKING FAMILY

The Rothschild banking family is the subject of countless conspiracy theories, rumours, accusations and slander. All harness one of the oldest hatreds in history, that of Jews, and combine it with the speed and truth vacuum that the internet provides. Among the accusations against the Rothschilds are that they control most of the world's money supply, are involved in dark rituals and devil worship, that they've manipulated the economies of almost every nation on Earth, and have started countless wars while funding all of the participants – all to slake their limitless thirst for wealth and power.

But conspiracy theories aside, the Rothschilds do have a long history of successfully investing around the world. They also were, for quite some time, the most prominent face of Jewish wealth. And much of it has been done in secret, with huge amounts of money moving through mysterious corporations that are held only by family members. So what's the truth about the Rothschild conspiracy, and what's just conspiracy?

'I CARE NOT WHO MAKES THE LAWS'

The Rothschilds amassed the world's largest private fortune in the 19th century, with a line beginning at dynasty founder Mayer Amschel Rothschild and continuing through his five sons, sent to the financial centres of Europe. The insular nature of the family gave it an aura of mystery and impenetrability. And in the deeply anti-Semitic Europe of the 18th and 19th centuries, that's all it took for a parallel pseudo-history to be born.

According to various accusations, the Rothschilds control as much as 80 per cent of the money supply of the world, building a fortune through a ruthless investing, dark manipulation and massive rigging of world events. Much of the early lore about the Rothschild family concerns their role in the Battle of Waterloo, particularly Mayer's son Nathan. It became a legend in Europe that Nathan invested in both sides of the battle, fooling the rest of Europe into losing a fortune, and even quipping 'buy when there's blood in the streets, even if the blood is your own'. But the most famous quote of the Rothschilds comes from Mayer himself, long held to have remarked 'give me control of a nation's money supply, and I care not who makes its laws'.

The Rothschilds were said to have invested massively in both sides of the Napoleonic Wars, the American Civil War, the Franco-Prussian War and World Wars I and II. When any leader got in their way, such as Abraham Lincoln or John F. Kennedy, the Rothschilds simply had them killed. They are said to control countless puppet leaders, including Hitler, born of Mayer's son Salomon and an Austrian housekeeper. The Rothschilds are even alleged to have orchestrated the Holocaust, to push for the founding of Israel.

Through it all, the Rothschilds have been buying up central banks around the world, with only a few outliers such as Iran, Russia and North Korea subject to a constant string of Western aggression. All of this market manipulation has given the Rothschilds a fortune that some conspiracy theorists peg at 500 trillion dollars. And it's invested in vast estates where the family delights in human sacrifice to Moloch, hunting people for sport, Satanic rituals, masked balls where no outsiders are allowed, and even cavorting with reptilian aliens. Any Rothschild member who objects is murdered through staged suicide, as the family consolidates its power and stamps out anyone who would get in its way.

MORE WEALTH THAN EXISTS ON EARTH

Conspiracy theories about the Rothschild family began almost as soon as Mayer Amschel Rothschild began building his fortune. As conspiracy author and sceptic Brian Dunning puts it, 'Their history is perhaps largely responsible for the modern belief that Jews control the world's money supply.' In Medieval Europe, Jews were forbidden from owning property, and were often pushed into occupations considered 'inferior' or sinful, such as money-lending, tax collection and banking. In particular, Jews were allowed to do one critical thing Christians weren't: charge interest. This divide allowed Jews to amass large fortunes through lending and recouping interest, and keep it in their own banks, hiding and moving money as needed.

Mayer Rothschild was the founder of the extraordinarily wealthy and successful Rothschild dynasty.

The Rothschilds were said to have made their fortune by investing in both sides of the Battle of Waterloo.

Mayer Amschel Rothschild excelled at this, building up enough of a fortune to do business dealings with the nobility of Germany. Rothschild supplied coins to the future Crown Prince of Hesse, Wilhelm, eventually becoming his personal banker, and investing Wilhelm's fortune to the point where he became the richest man in Europe. Mayer then acted as a go-between for England and Hesse in the hiring of mercenaries to fight in the American Revolution. By the time Napoleon invaded Hesse in the early 1800s, sending Crown Prince Wilhelm into exile, Mayer had already sent his five sons to the five major financial centres of Europe to continue expanding the rapidly growing family fortune.

By the 1900s, the Rothschilds had rescued the Bank of England from a liquidity crisis, were often called upon to stabilize struggling central banks, had

Wilhelm I of Hesse employed Mayer Rothschild as his personal banker.

financed the building of the Suez Canal, invested massively in some of the most desirable real estate in Europe, held diamond and mineral mines, and had vast sums of money invested in railroads, art, wine and asset management. But does this all add up to the '$500 trillion' amount that conspiracy theorists allege? No, because that number represents more money than the entirety of the gross domestic product of the world. The accusation that they control '80 per cent of the world's money supply' is also massively overinflated. Both of these numbers appear to have been made up, and have no supporting documentation. In fact, there is no individual Rothschild in the top 1,000 on Forbes' list of richest people.

Many of the conspiracy theories about the Rothschilds' history are based on wilful misunderstandings of complex concepts in banking. There are no 'Rothschild central banks', because a central bank is a government-owned financial instrument that sets fiscal policy and prints money, not a private institution. Nor did the Rothschilds 'take over' the Bank of England, as many conspiracy theorists allege, merely make a loan that was repaid. Nathan Rothschild did not manipulate the Battle of Waterloo to profit off both sides, while fooling investors into thinking England had lost (a bit of folklore that comes from a Nazi-era movie). He merely was able to get the news of England's victory quickly, then bought British government bonds – correctly calculating that they'd spike in value. And there's no evidence the family has 'funded both sides' of every major war, nor that they have the wealth to do so.

The vast majority of the other accusations, such as Hitler being a descendant of the Rothschilds, or the family holding human sacrifices at their estates, or assassinating John Kennedy, are simply rumours created and spread by anti-Semites. Some originate with the Nazis, others with the modern internet conspiracy movement. Even the quote so often attributed to Mayer Amschel Rothschild, the one that casts the family as manipulators of world events for profit, is apocryphal, with no primary source.

The modern Rothschild family is still wealthy and

secretive, but also philanthropic and vocal about the causes it supports. It's divided up between generations of members, with its original monopolies on lending long dissolved. Its estates have largely been sold off, its art given away. Much of the power it retains in the conspiracy community, then, comes thanks to the historical conspiracy theories about it, not anything it's currently doing.

ABOVE: The Rothschilds provided the funding for one of the most ambitious projects of the late nineteenth century, the building of the Suez Canal.

BELOW: The Schloss Hinterleiten was one of many palaces built by the Rothschilds. In 1905 the family donated it to charity, reflecting a tendency towards philanthropy that continues to this day.

THE NEW WORLD ORDER

Many conspiracy theories feature the power elite uniting to exploit those deemed to be 'useless eaters' – those requiring help from society but giving nothing back. The one known as the 'New World Order', popular in the 1990s but still very much a going concern in the conspiracy community, is more plausible than most because it has roots in very real geopolitical events. Politicians and statesmen have continuously been trying to remake the twentieth-century world in their image, tossing out the old ways of war and ushering in a new order based on peace and equality. Some of the greatest minds of the last hundred years have tried to push society towards what they deemed a 'new world order', and these proposals have been twisted and reinterpreted by conspiracy theorists as something much darker – moving the planet away from freedom and self-determination and towards globalization and central control. Mass surveillance, global government, the purging of dissenters, mind control, planned economies feeding into one socialist system, and even the fulfilment of biblical end times prophecies are all key components to the conspiracy theory version of a 'new world order'.

Woodrow Wilson helped create the idea of a 'new world order' through the 'Fourteen Points' he put forward after the end of World War I.

While some of what the New World Order conspiracy theory posits is interchangeable with other theories, it also stands on its own as a unique entity with a long history. Are we really forever standing at the precipice of world government and socialist slavery?

TOWARDS A NEW WORLD ORDER

There is a sizable difference between what politicians and authors have generally referred to as 'a new world order' and the specific proper noun 'the New World Order' of conspiracy theories. The first has no specific definition, while the second does. Statesmen have long sought to use international traumas like the World Wars as the jumping off point for a more peaceful and less atavistic global society. It was President Woodrow Wilson who first codified the idea of a new world order with his call for putting international cooperation ahead of nationalistic goals. Wilson's 'Fourteen Points' were a blueprint for a world ravaged by the Great War, where disputes could be settled without violence, including the creation of a 'general association of nations' that became known as the League of Nations.

Despite their good intentions, the United States rejected Wilson's ideas, with Theodore Roosevelt calling the Fourteen Points 'high-sounding and meaningless', and another US Senator calling the proposed League of Nations 'treacherous and treasonable'. It would not

be the last time that the concept of a 'new world order' was dismissed and insulted, with no less than Adolf Hitler referring to the League as a 'new world coalition' meant to cover for French militarism. Nonetheless, some versions of the Wilsonian new world order were revived again after World War II, leading to the United Nations, NATO and the International Monetary Fund.

But the most famous use of the phrase 'new world order' came in the aftermath of the Cold War. Sensing the opportunity to remake the world free of East vs West aggression, reformist Soviet premier Mikhail Gorbachev told the UN in a June 1990 speech that 'For a new type of progress throughout the world to become a reality, everyone must change,' and that 'tolerance is the alpha and omega of a new world order'. His counterpart, US President George H. W. Bush, echoed Gorbachev by telling a joint session of Congress in September that 'we can see a new world coming into view. A world in which there is the very real prospect of a new world order.' After Bush used the term, decades of conspiracies about some undetermined mass of power elites taking control of our world suddenly had a figurehead – and an agenda to be fought.

BLACK HELICOPTERS AND WACO

To conspiracy theorists, the New World Order Gorbachev and Bush were proposing wasn't defined by tolerance or peace, but by naked lust for power. In his 2010 book *The New World Order: Facts & Fiction*, conspiracy theorist author Mark Dice defines the New World Order as 'the plan to create a socialist global government headed up by one world leader and a wealthy ruling class [...] and render the rest of the world's population powerless.'

This wasn't new in conspiracy theory circles. Author Gary Allen had written several books using the phrase to label a globalist cabal working together to undermine the West. Other popular books in that same vein were John Stormer's *None Dare Call It Treason*, William Guy Carr's *The Red Fog Over America* and William Luther Pierce's *The Turner Diaries*. They all told of a powerful alliance of communists, Jews and the government working to destroy everything dear about America. The concept was also popular with paleo-conservative groups like the John Birch Society, as well as Christian millennialist movements, spurred by Pat Robertson's hugely popular 1991 book *The New World Order*. Robertson mashed a generation of conspiracy theories together, putting everyone from the Freemasons to New Age practitioners to Wall Street bankers in a vast plot to

George H. W. Bush was another leading statesman to talk of the creation of a new world order.

Black helicopters loaded with armed government thugs have become the fearful image of the supposed New World Order.

enslave free people under the eye of a tyrannical world government. In the conspiracy crazed first years of Bill Clinton's presidency, New World Order fever was all over AM radio, the nascent internet, American churches and TVs, and books sold at gun shows and surplus stores. Talk radio hosts fretted about black helicopters and jackbooted FBI thugs, while anti-government militias armed up, Mulder and Scully tangled with conspiracies and monsters on *The X-Files*, and televangelists preached that societal collapse was only one UN initiative away.

It didn't help that the Clinton administration was involved in several incidents that New World Order believers saw as portends of things to come: the burning of the Branch Davidians compound in Waco, Texas; and the shooting of Aryan Nation member Randy Weaver's wife and son by ATF agents. There were also multiple new laws seen as an unacceptable rollback of gun rights, including the Brady Handgun Violence Prevention Act of 1993, which mandated federal background checks and waiting periods, and the much-derided Assault Weapons Ban of a year later. But the crescendo of organized opposition to the New World Order came on 19 April 1995. Conspiracy theorists Timothy McVeigh and Terry Nichols were hardcore believers in the New World Order, and inspired by the disaster at Waco, they sought to fight back against what they believed was a

local headquarters of the nefarious organization: the Alfred P. Murrah Federal Building in Oklahoma City. McVeigh and Nichols built a gigantic truck bomb, and McVeigh detonated it, killing 168 people, including a number of children. The uprising that the two men hoped to provoke never took place, and the anti-government militia movement was eviscerated by the FBI in the wake of the attack.

With that, belief in the New World Order suddenly became a lot less trendy and acceptable, with many believers moving on to other conspiracy theories – some related to the US government, and some not. But even though the idea of a named and organized 'New World Order' has fallen out of favour in the movement, the concept of a world-controlling, string-pulling cabal is still very much a going concern. The modern idea of the deep state relies on the same combination of end-of-the-world prophecy, fear of government overreach, relentless fear-based grifting, and cabalistic bankers engineering world events that the New World Order did. And while that movement was stopped by the backlash to the Oklahoma City bombing, the modern deep state has had no such incident to dim its popularity. At least, not yet.

The Oklahoma City bombing in 1995 was conducted by Timothy McVeigh, a firm believer in the New World Order conspiracy theory.

CHAPTER 4

POLITICAL CONSPIRACIES

Of all the varieties of conspiracy theory which abound, the most readily believed are perhaps those involving politicians, whatever their party allegiance. One reason for this may be the number of political cover-up theories which have been demonstrated to be true. This section opens with the grandaddy of all political scandals: the Watergate Affair.

WATERGATE

The Watergate Affair is one of the key conspiracy tales of our time. Not because it is the most outlandish or extraordinary of conspiracies, but because it turned out to be true. What began as a simple burglary turned out to be a scandal that forced the resignation of a United States president. Here was a real conspiracy and it was uncovered layer by layer until the conspirators – all the way up to President Richard Nixon himself – had to resign or face criminal charges. And perhaps the most lasting effect of the episode was to make sure that conspiracy theorists could no longer simply be written off. Previous events like the assassination of John F. Kennedy now looked more suspicious than ever and

the conspiracy theorists, once described as crackpots, were all of a sudden 'experts'. Never again would the American public simply accept what it was told – even by its president.

The whole extraordinary business began in the early hours of 17 June 1972 at a hotel and office block complex called the Watergate building in Washington DC. On that day a security guard named Frank Wills noticed a piece of tape being used to hold open a door leading in from the parking garage. Wills removed it, but did not think much of it. He imagined that the cleaning team had perhaps left it there. However, when he returned soon afterwards to discover that someone

The Watergate complex, where the scandal unfolded.

had put another piece of tape on the door, he decided to call the police. He told them that he suspected that a burglary might be in progress.

The police showed up and at 2.30 a.m. they found five men hiding in an office in the part of the building occupied by the Democratic National Committee. The five men were arrested and were found to include two Cubans, two men with CIA connections and a man named James W. McCord Jr, who was employed as Chief of Security at a Republican organization called the Committee to Re-elect the President. Alarm bells quickly started to ring. This was clearly no ordinary burglary but a politically motivated one.

Then it emerged that this was not the first Watergate break-in. The same team had already broken into the Democratic Campaign HQ and planted bugs there. Part of the reason for their return was to fix some wiretaps that were not working properly. Further alarm bells went off when the telephone number of one E. Howard Hunt was found in McCord's notebook. Hunt was a former White House consultant and CIA employee.

JUST A THIRD-RATE BURGLARY?

As news of the break-in made its way into the press, questions began to be asked about who in the White

A walkie talkie used in the Watergate break-in.

WATERGATE SCANDAL

Kleindienst

Haldeman

Ehrlichman

Magruder

Gray

Dean

Graphic showing the key players in the Watergate Affair, including President Richard Nixon (centre) and White House counsel John Dean (right).

House might have known of it. On 19 June *The Washington Post* reported that a Republican security aide was among the Watergate burglars. The former attorney general John Mitchell, head of the Nixon re-election campaign, denied any link with the operation and the White House did its best to play down the significance of the affair. Nixon press secretary Ron Ziegler called it a 'third-rate burglary' and the American public found it hard to accept that a president like Nixon – who was way ahead in all the opinion polls – would sanction a wiretapping operation against his rivals. On 30 August Nixon claimed that White House counsel John Dean had conducted an investigation into the Watergate matter and concluded that no one from the White House was involved. Nevertheless, press speculation refused to go away.

At his 5 September indictment, James McCord

identified himself as retired from the Central Intelligence Agency. The Washington DC district attorney's office began an investigation into the links between McCord and the CIA, and so too did a couple of young journalists from *The Washington Post*, Bob Woodward and Carl Bernstein. They started to dig deep, aided by leaks from a mysterious anonymous source, known only as 'Deep Throat'.

During the weeks leading up to the November election *The Washington Post* ran stories reporting that John Mitchell, while serving as attorney general, controlled a secret Republican fund that was used to finance widespread intelligence-gathering operations against the Democrats. Then it reported that FBI agents knew that the Watergate break-in was part of a massive campaign of political spying and sabotage that was being conducted on behalf of the Nixon re-election effort. Still the public took no notice and Nixon was duly re-elected by a landslide.

On 8 January 1973 the original burglars, along with Hunt and another former intelligence operative turned White House security consultant named Gordon Liddy, went to trial. All except McCord and Liddy pleaded guilty and all were convicted of conspiracy, burglary and wire tapping. The accused had been paid to plead guilty but say nothing and their refusal to confess to the crimes angered the trial judge John Sirica (known as 'Maximum John' because of his harsh sentencing). Sirica handed down 30-year sentences, but indicated that he would reconsider if the group would be more co-operative. McCord capitulated and wrote a letter to the judge in which he claimed that the defendants had pleaded guilty under duress. He said they had committed perjury at the urging of John Dean, counsel to the president, and John Mitchell, when he was the attorney general.

SECRET TAPES

By now the 'third-rate burglary' had become a major scandal. The revelations just kept coming. On 6 April John Dean, the White House Counsel, began co-operating with the Watergate prosecutors. Nixon

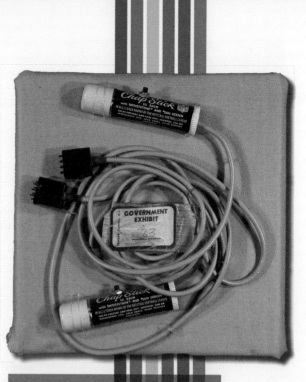

The Nixon administration bugged everyone. These chapstick tubes contained hidden microphones to record nearby conversations.

The tape recorder from Nixon's oval office.

A protest against Nixon on 22 October 1973.

9 August 1974: Nixon at the White House with his family after his resignation as president.

promised fresh investigations but began to look like a man engaged in a desperate cover-up. Dean was sacked and other presidential advisers were forced to resign, but the press were still not satisfied. Dean testified that he had mentioned the Watergate break-in to the president 35 times. Nixon denied it. But then the existence of tapes that contained all of the president's conversations in the Oval Office was discovered.

Nixon at first refused to release the tapes, but then handed over edited transcripts. Legal moves eventually forced him to hand over the original tapes, but parts of them were discovered to have been erased. Finally, Congress began to consider an extraordinary move – to impeach the president. At first this seemed impossible but then, with the August 1974 discovery of the 'smoking gun' tape that proved that Nixon knew of the cover-up operation, the impeachment process looked certain to go ahead. On 8 August Nixon accepted that the game was up and announced his resignation.

And so the most sensational conspiracy case in American history came to its end. Or did it? Today, there are any number of revisionist Watergate theories out there. Some say that the Democrats deliberately set Nixon up. Others suggest that Dean himself was responsible for the whole business and had ordered the break-in to cover up a prostitution scandal in which he was allegedly implicated.

In the final analysis though, it seems that the conspiracy theorists should learn to quit while they are ahead. Watergate was a conspiracy and it went all the way to the top. The guilty parties were even punished for it. What more satisfying end to a major conspiracy could there possibly be?

THE IRAN–CONTRA CONSPIRACY

US Marine Colonel Oliver North testifies during the Iran–Contra Congressional Hearings, during which he admitted selling arms to Iran to fund Nicaraguan Contras.

One of the most notorious conspiracies of the Reagan administration was the Iran–Contra affair, in which the United States government sold arms to Iran (supposedly an enemy state), and also funded anti-Communist forces, known as the Contras, in Nicaragua. Both the Iranian and the Nicaraguan activities were not only against declared United States government policy but were also in contravention of laws passed by Congress. When the activities were exposed, there was a scandal and several important figures were indicted, including Lieutenant-Colonel Oliver North, a key military official and John Poindexter, National Security Adviser under Ronald Reagan. President Reagan himself was forced to make an appearance on television to explain his actions to the American public. He maintained that he considered what he had done to be right and he survived the scandal, but it damaged the reputation of his administration considerably.

DOUBLE DEALING

At the time that the scandal broke, in the mid-1980s, Nicaragua was in the midst of a civil war between the Marxist government, known as the Sandinistas, and their opponents, the anti-Communist Contras, who were engaged in guerrilla warfare. The country's proximity to the United States meant that they were always vulnerable to influence from their powerful neighbour and it was clear that the United States was opposed to the Marxist government in power there. However, the fact that the United States was funding the Contras, in the hope that they could topple the left-wing government, did not become public knowledge for some time. Even more shocking, it later transpired that the money that was used to fund the Contras had come from the sale of American arms to Iran, which at the time was being run by an Islamic fundamentalist government and was ostensibly an enemy of the United

Contra soldiers in 1987. These anti-Communist forces in Nicaragua were supported by the US in the hopes that they would topple the left-wing ruling government of the country.

States. What came out was that the Americans were hoping that the sale of arms to Iran would persuade the Iranians to intercede with Islamic terrorists in Lebanon, who were holding hostages there. However, this double dealing was completely against international law and was also hypocritical since, in public, President Reagan was critical of the regime in Iran.

ARMS FOR HOSTAGES

To solve the problem of how to get the hostages back, a secret deal was made in which arms were sold to Iran in exchange for the release of the hostages in Lebanon. The proposal for the plan came from the Israeli government, who suggested that the United States should broker a deal to sell hundreds of missiles to Iran, which at the time was fighting the Iran–Iraq war. The missiles were designed to defeat armoured tanks and they boasted important new features, including laser range-finders and thermal optics. In exchange, the terrorists in Lebanon that were holding Benjamin Weir, an American hostage, would release their captive.

The deal took place under the direction of Defense Secretary Caspar Weinberger and the first American hostage was freed in September. Two months later, a similar transaction took place in which 500 Hawk anti-aircraft missiles were to be shipped to Iran. The purpose of the Hawk missiles was to shoot down aircraft and they could be launched from the ground into the air by a single soldier. However, the cost of these missiles was so high that the proposal needed to go through

Congress. Robert McFarlane, the president's national security adviser, pressed for the deal to go ahead and, in 1985, the first shipment of missiles reached Iran. Negotiations continued into 1986, setting out a new deal in which an intermediary, Manucher Ghorbanifar, would sell arms to Iran in exchange for the hostages.

However, the plan began to founder when, after releasing their hostages, the terrorists began to take new ones. Also, Ghorbanifar and Colonel Oliver North, the aide to Reagan's national security adviser, were accused of selling the weapons at highly inflated prices.

FUNDING THE CONTRAS

It later emerged that the money made from the sale of arms to Iran was being used to fund the Nicaraguan Contras in their bid to oust the democratically elected government there.

Earlier in the decade, a scandal had broken when it was discovered that the CIA were secretly providing help to the Contras and legislation, under the Boland Amendment of 1982, had been drawn up to prevent this happening again. However, National Security Adviser John Poindexter and his aide Oliver North had managed to find a legal loophole. They conducted their business under the auspices of the National Security Council, which was not subject to the Boland Amendment.

It was just a matter of time before the press discovered what was going on and blew the whistle on the scandal. The arms for hostages deal was exposed in

A Hawk anti-air missile in flight.

President Reagan meets with his aides over the Iran–Contra affair.

1986, after an incident in which it was discovered that guns were being smuggled into Nicaragua for use by the Contras. Oliver North and Fawn Hall, his secretary, came under scrutiny after they destroyed documents concerning the deal. The administration was eventually forced to admit what had happened.

FINDING THE CULPRITS

In order to allay criticism, President Reagan ordered a commission, later known as the Tower Commission, to look into the problem. He alleged that he had no idea that arms were being exchanged for hostages and that the profits from the arms were being used to support the Contras in Nicaragua. The Commission named North and Poindexter, mentioned that Weinberger was also involved and suggested that the president should have been more aware of the activities of his staff. In 1987, Congress indicted McFarlane, Poindexter and

North and they were convicted on several counts, but these convictions were later overturned. Reagan himself survived the scandal, although it became clear, as information emerged, that he had been involved in the deals, at least to some degree.

The Iran–Contra conspiracy remains one of the biggest scandals to emerge under the Reagan administration. It showed how top government officials acted with no regard for Congressional or international law. They made up their own rules in a secret political game, both within and outside America, that flouted the conventions of democracy and fair play. The fact that all the players in the game were ultimately pardoned has caused many commentators to suggest that conspiracy continues to lie at the heart of the Machiavellian business of government – not just of totalitarian states, but of our great democracies as well.

THE CIA AND

There are many conspiracy theories about the CIA and its involvement in destabilizing left-wing regimes in foreign countries around the world. Some of them are difficult to take seriously and are born of sheer paranoia, while others seem credible but are difficult to prove. However, in the case of the overthrow of Salvador Allende in the Chilean coup of 1973, it is clear that the CIA ran a covert operation over a number of years in order to undermine the popularity of the democratically elected president. It is also apparent that it was involved in the events that led to his downfall.

THE RISE OF ALLENDE

Born in Valparaiso, Chile, in 1903, Salvador Allende studied medicine and became involved in radical politics while still a student. In 1933, he helped set up the Chilean Socialist Party, whose aim was

Salvador Allende, the left-wing Prime Minister who ruled Chile from 1970 until he was overthrown in the coup of 1973.

SALVADOR ALLENDE

to pursue Marxist policies outside the influence of the Soviet Union. He became Minister of Health in 1939 in the government of Aguirre Cedra before becoming a senator. After that he ran for president, finally achieving office in 1970, after three unsuccessful attempts.

As the new president, Allende pledged to solve Chile's pressing economic and social problems. At the time of his presidency, inflation and unemployment had reached drastic proportions and over half of the country's children were suffering from malnutrition. Allende immediately introduced wage increases, froze prices, nationalized the banking and copper industries and began to institute land reforms. This made him extremely unpopular with the United States, which had wide-ranging corporate interests in Chile.

THE COUP

In September 1970, President Richard Nixon instructed Henry Kissinger, the American Secretary of State, to support a coup against Allende's socialist government in Chile. Kissinger now claims that although he initially followed the president's orders, he and the CIA later ceased to be involved in the plot. Three years later, there actually was a military coup in Chile which removed Allende and his government from power and installed General Augustus Pinochet as president instead. Allende is thought to have committed suicide during the fighting, by shooting himself with a gun given to him by Fidel Castro.

General Pinochet went on to rule Chile as an authoritarian dictator until 1990 and during his

The authoritarian dictator Augusto Pinochet took over after the coup.

The bombing of the Chilean presidential palace in 1973.

regime he became notorious for human rights abuses. Kissinger and the CIA were accused of being involved in those abuses during that time. They purportedly assisted in the organization of 'Operation Condor', a secret, right-wing military group that kidnapped and murdered hundreds of the regime's political opponents throughout the 1970s.

CIA INVOLVEMENT?

It has now been proved that from 1963 to 1973 the CIA did its utmost to prevent a socialist government from gaining power in Chile. During the 1964 elections they helped pay expenses for the opposition. They also ran national propaganda campaigns on radio, TV and in the press with the object of demonstrating that Allende's communist policies would ruin the country. Six years later, in the presidential election of 1970, the agency conducted a campaign against Allende himself. Despite this, however, Allende went on to win the election by a narrow margin. After that, the CIA tried to persuade other Chilean politicians to tamper with the political process in order to oust the newly ensconced president, even to the point of organizing a coup. When that

also failed, the United States began to exert economic pressure on the country.

In addition to his enemies in the United States, Allende had plenty of opponents in Chile itself, people who stood to lose wealth and power as a result of his policies. Moreover, the change in the political direction of the country had caused a number of economic and social problems, which were exacerbated by the hostile stance of the United States. In particular there was a strong current of opposition against Allende within the military, and it was from this quarter that the coup of 1973 was mounted against him.

Today, it is still unclear to what degree the CIA were involved in organizing the coup. There is no doubt, however, that some form of covert action took place in Chile during Allende's years in office and that the CIA was still continuing its campaign against him at the time of the coup.

PROJECT FUBELT

Numerous investigations have helped clarify the role of the United States in the Chilean coup, although some believe that the full truth has yet to come

Henry Kissinger meets with President Nixon. Even if he did not directly plan the coup, it appears that Nixon did what he could to help it succeed.

out. Former Secretary of State Henry Kissinger has admitted that although Nixon did not have a direct hand in the coup, he 'created the conditions as great as possible' for it. Also, according to recently declassified documents, the United States government tried to oust Allende under 'Project Fubelt' in 1970. At that time, the CIA had links with General Roberto Viaux, who was planning a coup against the president which involved kidnapping the army chief of staff General René Schneider. (Schneider opposed the idea of military intervention on constitutional grounds.) The coup misfired in an episode that led to the death of General Schneider.

Afterwards, Kissinger maintained that the CIA had withdrawn from the plot. There is still no hard evidence to connect the CIA with the subsequent coup in 1973, but its involvement in this earlier attempt naturally fuels suspicion. It has also been pointed out that much of the information remains classified. In recent years, it has also become clear that although the United States government publicly criticized Pinochet, the CIA supported the military junta and paid many of the officers to become informants. Some of these officers,

it has been alleged, were party to human rights abuses, although the CIA has denied this claim.

AFTERMATH

Victims of the Pinochet regime have now begun to take legal action against the United States government and the CIA. In 2001, the family of General René Schneider accused Kissinger of plotting to murder the general because of his opposition to the military coup. It was discovered that although the CIA had discussed kidnapping Schneider they had not intended to kill him. Kissinger maintained that he and Nixon had decided not to back the coup at the last minute.

Whatever the truth of the matter, it remains clear that over a number of years the role of the CIA in Chile was to undermine the career of Salvador Allende and prevent the success of a socialist government by means of a series of underhand dealings with his opponents.

The CIA eventually achieved its aim – but the popular image of the United States as a protector of democracy was compromised. Thus, in the case of Chile, the conspiracy theorists were proved right.

CHAPPAQUI

The three Kennedy brothers dominated the American political landscape during the 1960s and each one of them was involved in a sensational news story that in turn led to a whole range of conspiracy theories. In the case of the two elder brothers, John and Robert, the sensational events were their assassinations. However, their younger brother, Edward 'Teddy' Kennedy, hit the headlines because of the death of a young woman named Mary Jo Kopechne.

Mary Jo Kopechne was 28 years old at the time of her death. She had worked in Washington since graduating from college, first as secretary to Senator George Smathers and then to Robert Kennedy. During Kennedy's presidential campaign she had become part of a devoted and hardworking team known as the 'boiler room girls'. Following Robert Kennedy's assassination in 1968 the 'boiler room girls' had been busy closing up his office. As a way of thanking them for their hard work, Robert's brother Edward Kennedy, also a Senator, had invited them to spend a weekend at Martha's Vineyard. They would watch a yachting race at Edgartown on 18 July 1969 and then a party would be held in their honour on Chappaquiddick island.

The bridge at Chappaquiddick were the incident occurred.

CRASHED OVER BRIDGE

The party was a small affair. The six 'boiler room girls' all attended – Kopechne, Susan Tannenbaum, Maryellen Lyons, Nance Lyons, Rosemary (Cricket) Keough and Esther Newburgh – and the other guests were six men, all of them married but without their wives in attendance. The men were Edward Kennedy, US Attorney Paul Markham, Joe Gargan (Kennedy's cousin and lawyer), Charles Tretter, Raymond La Rosa and John Crimmins. Gargan rented the venue, called Lawrence Cottage, and John Crimmins supplied the alcohol. He brought three half gallons of vodka, four fifths of scotch, two bottles of rum and two cases of beer

– an ample amount for 12 people, when at least two of them were not drinking.

According to Kennedy's account, what happened next was that Kennedy offered to drive Kopechne home at around 11.15 p.m., a journey that involved catching the ferry from the island back to Edgartown. Unfortunately, instead of turning left on to the road to the ferry he turned right and found himself on an unfamiliar road that led him unexpectedly to a narrow bridge. The car crashed over the side of the bridge and fell into the water, turning over in the process.

STATE OF SHOCK

At first Kennedy thought he was going to drown but then the door burst open and he was carried to the surface. He looked around for Kopechne but he could not see her. Although he dived down, the current was

ODICK

Mary Jo Kopechne – victim of a car accident or something more sinister?

too strong and he was unable to get into the car to save her. Suffering from concussion and shock, he made his way back to the cottage where he enlisted the help of Gargan and Markham. They returned to the car and tried again to dive down, still without success. Still in a state of shock, Kennedy returned to the ferry landing and swam across to the mainland, where he returned to his hotel. It was only in the morning that he came to his senses and called the police to report the accident.

This account was more or less accepted by the police. Kennedy was summoned to court to answer the charge of either failing to remain at the scene of an accident he had caused or at least failing to report it. He was let off with a two-month suspended sentence for this crime, despite the fact that the law appeared to state that the offence should carry a mandatory jail sentence. Throughout the proceedings, Kennedy maintained that

he had not been drunk at the time of the accident. By the following day, of course, it was impossible to check whether he was telling the truth or not.

AN AFFAIR?

Unsurprisingly, many people had a hard time believing Kennedy's version of events and before long evidence began to appear that magnified those doubts. A local deputy sheriff, Christopher 'Huck' Look, had returned home a little after 12.30 on the night in question and had remembered seeing a car with a man and a woman in it parked close to the point at which the road to the cottage met the main road. Look thought that the occupants might be lost so he got out of his car to offer help. As he approached, the car reversed fast and headed down the road, actually little more than a dirt track, that led to the fateful bridge.

A diver investigates Edward Kennedy's battered car in the Willamette River following the accident.

If the car was indeed Kennedy's then the incident casts immediate doubt on the story that he was driving Kopechne to the ferry, because the last boat had left by then. What many suspect is that Kennedy had rather more in mind than a simple lift home for Kopechne and that they were in fact deliberately heading down the dirt road to the nearby beach for a romantic assignation. According to this theory, what then happened was that the appearance of the sheriff panicked Kennedy, who might well have been intoxicated. This perhaps caused him to drive too fast down the dirt road so that he ploughed straight off the side of the bridge.

Further doubts have been cast over Kennedy's story that he was too shocked to report the accident. For instance, there were houses near the bridge where he could have asked for help. Instead he made his way to the cottage and called on the assistance of the two men most likely to be discreet, Gargan and Markham. According to Gargan's subsequent testimony, the first thing on Kennedy's mind, even before the fate of Kopechne, was how to cover up his role in the accident. He allegedly told Gargan that they should say that

Kopechne herself had been driving the car alone. After Gargan had told him that the plan was potentially disastrous an angered Kennedy then swam off back to his hotel. There he went to bed. He emerged the next day looking fit and well dressed and not at all like a man in shock. It was only when Gargan and Markham came over on the ferry that morning that they persuaded him that he did indeed have to report the accident.

SUFFOCATED NOT DROWNED

By that time the sunken car had been spotted and diver John Farrar had found the dead body of Kopechne inside. Chillingly, he reported that her posture suggested that she had been caught in an air pocket and had suffocated when the air had run out. She had apparently not drowned. This judgement was allegedly supported by the undertaker who worked on her body, although no autopsy was performed that would have verified the cause of her death. If Farrar was right, however, and Kopechne had been held in an air pocket, it is possible that she may have remained alive for as long as two hours after the crash. In that case it is conceivable that

Senator Edward Kennedy (right) with his brothers Jack and Robert at Hyannisport, Massachusetts.

Kennedy's failure to raise the alarm may have brought about her death.

It is harsh, but not unreasonable, to suspect that Kennedy may have valued his career rather more than Kopechne's life. If so, he was only partially successful. The scandal was not enough to force him to resign his Senatorship but it did put paid to his chances of ever becoming president, his greatest ambition.

There are definite elements of conspiracy in the events surrounding the prosecution of the affair. In particular, Kennedy's history of driving offences was mysteriously absent from the records that were given to the court. There are also those who see a larger conspiracy here. These theorists believe that the whole business was a set-up that was designed to discredit Kennedy. According to this theory, the CIA (or perhaps a shadowy organization known as the Power Control Group) had already assassinated John and Robert Kennedy, but realized that it would look too suspicious if they assassinated Edward as well. However, by setting up the Kopechne debacle they might be able to ruin his reputation instead.

The theories get frankly sketchy when a method needs to be found. In essence, they suggest that Kennedy was either drugged at the party or waylaid and knocked out. Then he was taken back to his hotel room unconscious – which explains why he never reported the accident. Meanwhile, the CIA drugged or knocked out Kopechne, positioned the car near the bridge, wedged the gas pedal down and launched her to her watery grave. The main problem with this theory is the role of Kennedy himself. On waking up the next morning why wouldn't he have revealed what really happened?

The answer the conspiracy theorists offer is that he was blackmailed, that the CIA threatened to tell his pregnant wife that he was having an affair with Kopechne. This is a pretty thin explanation, however. If Kennedy was so easy to blackmail, there would have been no need to fix up such an elaborate and risky scheme as the one that involved Mary Jo Kopechne. Overall then, it seems likely that the only real conspiracy was the one launched by Kennedy in an attempt to save his career.

FALSE FLAG

One of the central concepts of the modern conspiracy movement is that the governments of the world are constantly using faked incidents and terrorist attacks to push their agenda upon the rest of us. So virtually every time a shooting, bombing or car attack takes place somewhere in the world, the term 'false flag' is applied to it – taking a real military term for attacking under a false identity and applying it far past its defined usage.

Conspiracy theory sites are full of lists of 'admitted' false flag attacks, including everything from Nero's burning of Rome and faked Nazi aggression implicating Poland as a pretext for war, to the 11 September attacks and the Boston Marathon bombing. Such long lists of perceived conspiracy theories are usually easily dismissed as fallacious arguments for events that can't be proven. Except for one inconvenient fact: many of these listed incidents are actually false flags, and we know they are. In fact, the use of disguises and trickery as a pretext for military action has been either the real or hypothesized kick-off event for some of the most destructive military conflicts in human history.

REAL FALSE FLAGS – FROM MUKDEN TO MOSCOW

The term 'false flag' originated with naval warfare, when a ship would run up a flag other than its designated battle ensign in order to draw an enemy ship closer – then run up its real battle flag (fighting while actually pretending to be your enemy being against the rules of war) and open fire, catching the enemy unprepared.

During the World Wars, the allies made extensive use of 'Q-Ships', military ships disguised as unarmed merchant vessels designed to lure enemy ships closer. Another example was the 1942 British raid on the German-held dock at St Nazaire, France, when the Royal Navy rebuilt an old destroyer to look like a German patrol boat, then sailed it under a German flag to get close enough to the dock to blow it up.

These tactics were also common during land warfare, such as the famous German plan to use English-speaking commandos dressed in American uniforms to carry out sabotage behind Allied lines during the Battle of the Bulge. While most of these men were shot upon capture, the operation itself was later declared to be legal because the action didn't order them to actually fight while pretending to be Americans.

False flags also include attacks where soldiers of one country carry out an action against their own people in order to pin it on another country or group they want to go to war with. In fact, it was two false flags that

A British 'Q-ship' from World War I. Disguised as merchant vessels, 'Q-ships' would lure ships closer before opening fire, in an early example of 'false flag' attacks.

Japanese troops enter Northeast China after the Mukden Incident in 1931.

kicked off World War II – both extremely transparent, but just real enough to be useful.

Japan kicked off its 1931 invasion of Northeast China with a staged bombing of the Japanese-owned South Manchuria Railway, using a tiny explosive that was so ineffective that a train went over the railroad minutes later. But this fake attack, later called the 'Mukden Incident', was all the justification Japan needed to invade. The German invasion of Poland was also preceded by dozens of incidents involving German troops dressed in Polish uniforms carrying out random acts of vandalism, destruction and terror along the Germany/Poland border. After a slew of these faked attacks, Germany invaded Poland.

Many other famous false flags that led to military conflict have been long suspected as having been carried out by (or at least exploited by) the country that absorbed the attack. The 1898 sinking of the USS Maine by what was probably a coal explosion sent the United States to war with Spain over Cuba, while the Reichstag fire that allowed Adolf Hitler to suspend civil liberties in Nazi Germany has been blamed by a number of historians on the Nazis themselves, despite a Dutch communist being executed for the crime.

In more recent history, the Gulf of Tonkin incident in August 1964, where North Vietnamese patrol boats attacked an American destroyer, is often called a false flag. One attack was real, but a second reported attack several days later was likely only sailors shooting at shadows. Nevertheless, President Johnson used the two incidents as a pretext to begin bombing targets in North Vietnam. And the horrifying Moscow apartment

bombings in September 1999 that killed over 250 people ensured the election of Vladimir Putin, who quickly cited it to justify invading Chechnya – even after local police arrested FSB agents in the process of setting off one of the bombs.

FALSE FALSE FLAGS

These incidents, real and debated alike, are not the same definition that conspiracy theorists have for 'false flag'. To conspiracy believers, there is virtually no incident of any kind that's not staged by the powers that be to excuse aggressive actions against the population. Almost every American mass shooting of the last two decades has been labelled a government-planned false flag to strip away gun rights. The Sandy Hook shooting, the Pulse Nightclub massacre in Orlando, and the Las Vegas Strip attack in October 2017 were labelled as staged attacks minutes after they happened, fuelled by social media rumours of second shooters and faked victims.

The same holds true for attacks outside the United States. The London bombings of July 2007, Anders Brevik's massacre in Oslo in 2011, the 2015 Charlie Hebdo shooting and the Berlin Christmas market attack of 2016 were all deemed by conspiracy theorists to be government-concocted plots, carried out to advance draconian security measures, influence domestic policy or simply to strike terror into the people. It's understandable why conspiracy theorists look at these incidents and include them with the very real false flags of the past. After all, many did lead to draconian security measures and fear in the populace. But does that mean they were faked?

Flowers surround the Las Vegas sign in memory of those who died from the 2017 shootings.

Historical false flag attacks were carried out to meet narrow objectives. For example, the faked Polish aggression against Germany wasn't simply done to advance nebulous ideas of 'consolidating power' or 'taking away rights'. It was to justify a specific course of action against one nation. This is a hallmark of conspiracy theories – they are full of details, but usually in the support of something extremely vague and unclear.

The proof that these incidents were faked usually depends on evidence known to be either fake or taken completely out of context. They mistake a lack of known motivation for a greater sinister intent, particularly with mass shootings, where the killer often takes their own life, leaving behind little in the way of motive or explanation for their actions.

And while some of these incidents have resulted in new laws, most haven't – particularly when it comes to guns. If these shootings were faked by the US government to strip away gun rights, the government has failed every time. Gun access in America is just as easy as ever, and the country hasn't passed major gun legislation since the now-expired Assault Weapons Ban in 1994.

None of these shootings or attacks have ever been proven to have been carried out by that particular government. In most cases, they would involve conspiracies so massive and labour-intensive that they'd fall apart at once. Real false flags have eventually been proven with evidence – or at least involve a theory that's plausible. But the 'staged mass shooting' theory has never had any compelling evidence that's stood up to scrutiny, and few are plausible.

While it might be easier to believe that the rulers of the world send shooters into schools and planes into buildings, that doesn't mean it's true. And a historical event happening once doesn't mean it's happening every time. If everything is a false flag, then nothing is.

Conspiracy theorists argue that these mass shootings are conducted by government to turn the public against gun rights, yet assault rifles remain as widely available in the United States as ever.

Conspiracy theories about the United Nations have existed since the first meetings of the international body. Radical far-right elements like the John Birch Society have spent decades calling the organization a prelude to one-world government, a front for communism, a vehicle for the return of the Antichrist, an unholy alliance with some meddling foreign power (usually Jews), an earth-worshipping hippie cult, and a front for global genocide through vaccines.

These conspiracy theories, almost entirely propagated by American and European conservatives, see the UN as a bloated and useless bureaucracy bent on sucking up more power and controlling our food, water, air, politics, transportation and religion. In the end, its controllers will eradicate those deemed by them to be 'useless eaters' and plunder what's left for themselves.

Speculated plots about world government are not new, of course. They didn't even start with the UN. When the League of Nations was formed out of the ashes of World War I, isolationist Senator Henry Cabot Lodge gave a thunderous speech calling it a 'mongrel banner' and declared that if the United States became entangled in the affairs of Europe, it would 'destroy her power for good and endanger her very existence'.

But while these and subsequent conspiracy theories have drifted in and out of favour as the decades have gone on, the most prevalent one of the last decade has a firmly twenty-first-century origin. In fact, it revolves around humanity's transition into a new century, and even includes its name – Agenda 21.

A PLAN TO RADICALLY CHANGE HUMANITY?

Agenda 21 is a non-binding, unenforceable policy paper, developed in 1992 and signed by 178 countries, including the United States. Declaring that 'human beings… are entitled to a healthy and productive life in harmony with nature', Agenda 21 is a long-term plan for environmentally healthy development, more efficient use of land and resources, improved urban planning, promoting wellness, combating poverty and reducing our impact on the land and water.

Among its objectives are promoting international trade that takes account of the needs of developing countries, better data collection and research, enabling the poor to achieve sustainable livelihoods, encouraging greater efficiency in the use of energy and resources, meeting primary healthcare needs, and

The United Nations are at the centre of the conspiracy theory regarding Agenda 21.

UNITED NATIONS CONFERENCE ON ENVIRONMENT AND DEVELOPMENT

Rio de Janeiro 3–14 June 1992

At the Earth Summit in Rio de Janeiro, 1992, the UN met to discuss environmental issues. The outcome of the summit was the signing of Agenda 21, a plan for sustainable, environmentally friendly development.

reducing health risks from environmental pollution and hazards.

Agenda 21 has no penalties for non-compliance, no enforcement arm to ensure any element is carried out and no requirements for how it's implemented. You can put into practice some, all, or none of it. Most of it is carried out at the community level, and it's meant to be most impactful on local issues such as traffic and resource use, with no oversight from the United Nations. And the plan is available online in its entirety, in a variety of languages. The world signed on to Agenda 21, and began implementing these sound and evidenced policies.

But two decades later, it became an Obama-era lightning rod for conservatives already feeling the heat of liberal fascism breathing down their necks. A wide range of Republican governmental bodies, pundits, writers and voters see Agenda 21 as nothing less than a nightmarish vision of the future, a horror show of draconian regulations and population transfer where environmental impact will be put before human happiness. And that's just for the lucky ones who aren't eliminated – a figure that some conspiracy videos peg at 95 per cent of the population. In the end, the planet will be a barely populated playground for the elite, with the survivors turned into little more than slaves of the UN, worked to death to support the elite.

But even a cursory reading of Agenda 21 shows none of that. So why is there such a disconnect between the real Agenda 21 and the conspiracy theory version?

WHICH IS THE REAL AGENDA?

Despite Agenda 21 having been signed in the early 1990s, it had almost no real footprint in the conspiracy theory world until late 2011. That was the beginning of an almost unceasing drumbeat of paranoia from conservative media figure Glenn Beck, who spent hours on multiple media platforms declaring that Agenda 21 was a diabolical plan to destroy local communities and 'centralize control over all of human life on planet earth'.

Beck even wrote a 2012 book called *Agenda 21*, (or rather, he put his name on a book written by someone else and grabbed the bulk of the royalties) where America has been replaced by a fascist state called 'the Republic'. In the Republic, there is 'no president. No Congress. No Supreme Court. No freedom,' as the book's promotional blurb puts it. 'There are only the Authorities. Citizens have two primary goals in the new Republic: to create clean energy and to create new human life. Those who cannot do either are of no use to society.' The original book was described by its editor as an enjoyable dystopian novel, something akin to *The Handmaid's Tale*. But Beck's involvement

Glenn Beck, a conservative talk show host, decried Agenda 21 as a plan to establish control over everyone on the planet.

Ted Cruz based his 2016 Presidential campaign on opposition to Agenda 21.

sent it rocketing through the ranks of the conservative movement as a document to be taken seriously.

The Republican National Committee put language in the official 2012 election platform decrying Agenda 21 as a 'comprehensive plan of extreme environmentalism, social engineering and global political control'. Multiple state legislatures passed laws banning any kind of involvement with it. And local tea party groups began protesting at planning commission seminars, city council hearings, zoning boards and board of supervisors meetings. The impact of these protests was far from just symbolic. In 2012, voters in Georgia voted down a one-cent sales tax meant to shore up crumbling Atlanta roads, largely due to fear of it being tied to Agenda 21. Multiple other states scuttled plans for bike lanes and high-speed rail tracks, and major cities were prevented from tracking carbon emissions and electricity usage. During his successful Senate campaign, Texas' Ted Cruz ran on opposing Agenda 21 as a plan to 'abolish...golf courses, grazing pastures, and paved roads'.

Conspiracy theorists on social media even shared an 'Agenda 21 death map', supposedly showing all the areas in the US where the population would be culled.

IS ANY OF THIS HAPPENING?

Agenda 21 was passed in 1992 – and yet not a single UN apartment block has appeared, no populations have been culled and nobody's golf course has been confiscated. Virtually none of the nefarious bike lane and carbon tax plans that have been linked to it actually are related to it, and the hysteria mostly died down after the 2012 election. Many communities have quietly and readily put its recommendations into practice, with notable improvements in carbon emissions and traffic. The plan has gone through a number of iterations and alterations, and a follow-up plan called '2030 Agenda for Sustainable Development' was passed by 193 UN member states in 2015.

Of course, conspiracy theorists attached themselves to that plan as well, calling it 'global socialism' built around population control, curtailing of free travel and trade and the 'removal' of the Second Amendment. But the new version didn't catch fire the way Agenda 21 did, at least not at the local level. Opponents seemed to realize that if the UN actually had a plan to purge the population, they'd manage to get around to it at some point.

If the world is going to withstand climate change, it will require extensive adaptability and flexibility about resource use. Agenda 21 and its successors are a path towards that – and it's understandable that many will resist any sort of change brought about by the UN. Even if that change is positive.

CHAPTER 5

MYSTERIES AND THE UNKNOWN

Although nineteenth-century authors such as Jules Verne speculated on the subject of alien life-forms, it was not until the second half of the twentieth century that the existence of beings from other worlds became such a passionately held conviction. The questions remain: do such life-forms exist, have they travelled millions of light years to visit us, and are governments of the world in collusion to cover up these visits?

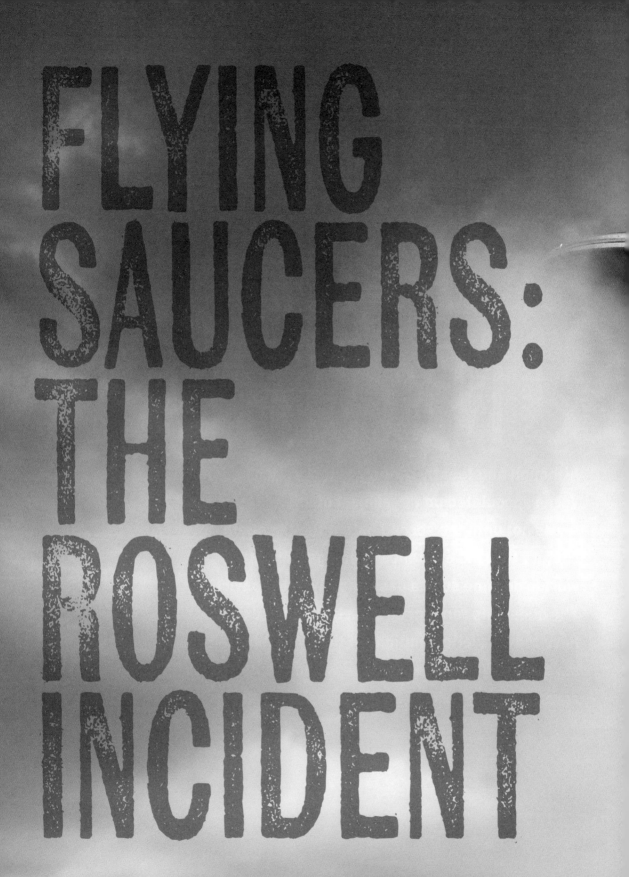

FLYING SAUCERS: THE ROSWELL INCIDENT

The Roswell Incident of June 1947 remains one of the most intriguing episodes in the history of UFO research. For many, it is the most persuasive evidence we have that alien beings exist, that they travel about the cosmos in spacecraft and that they once landed here on Earth.

The story began in 1947 when a pilot named Kenneth Arnold claimed that he had seen several objects flying 'like geese' through the sky near Mount Rainier, Washington. He described them 'moving like a saucer would if it skimmed across the water'. The journalist reporting the story coined the term 'flying saucer' to describe the craft and this has been used informally ever since to denote UFOs – unidentified flying objects.

Whether such objects exist, and whether Arnold was telling the truth when he made the claim that day, has been the subject of much speculation over the years. For what happened a few weeks afterwards confirmed, in many people's minds, that aliens had indeed visited our planet and that the American government, for reasons of its own, tried to hush up the story.

EXTRATERRESTRIAL CRASH LANDING?

In early July 1947, a rancher named William 'Mack' Brazel was riding out over land near Corona, New Mexico when he noticed a large amount of strange-looking debris scattered about. He informed Sheriff Wilcox of Chaves County who, thinking this must be to do with military exercises, passed the information on to the Army Air Force base at Roswell. Major Jesse Marcel, the base intelligence officer, was instructed to examine the debris. Meanwhile, a local newspaper published the story, reporting that a 'flying saucer' had landed on the ranch (they also claimed that it had 'been captured', which was a complete fabrication). The matter was then referred to the United States Army Air Force research laboratories, who issued a statement to the effect that

The story that launched a thousand saucers: the *Daily Record* of 8 July 1947 reports the Roswell 'incident'.

the debris was not a flying saucer but the remains of a high altitude weather balloon with a radar attachment made of aluminium and balsa wood, that was being used for State purposes.

After the sighting in New Mexico, the press picked up the story and many newspapers across the United States published more or less lurid accounts of it. Public interest ran high and various other sightings were reported during the summer of 1947. However, the army's insistence that the wreckage was not a crashed or captured flying saucer but simply the remains of a weather balloon eventually began to quell press and public interest in the subject.

THE EVIDENCE

The Roswell Incident, as it came to be called, looked destined to slip into obscurity for many years, but in 1978 a UFO researcher named Stanton Friedman began to delve into it once again. While on a lecture tour, he received a call from Jesse Marcel, who had handled the affair back in 1947. However, Marcel could not remember the date on which the incident took

place. With the help of co-researcher William Moore, Friedman began to find out more and eventually unearthed newspaper clippings reporting the story. Then the pair began to ask questions. What kind of weather balloon could yield such strange debris? Brazel and others had said that the material they had found was extremely light and could not be burned or otherwise destroyed. Why would they lie about such a thing? And why was the whole affair cloaked in such secrecy? The army seemed to have something to hide – what was it?

LITTLE GREEN MEN

Friedman and Moore interviewed a teletype operator named Lydia Sleppy. She had worked at a New Mexico radio station in 1947 and had claimed that the FBI had interrupted the transmission of the 'flying saucer' story. This seemed to tally with Marcel's account, in which he had stated that the army had suppressed information about the strange debris that he had seen with his own eyes and that the 'weather balloon' story had been a cover-up. A retired air force brigadier general called Arthur Exon then came out of the woodwork.

Jesse Marcel examines the debris from a supposed 'flying saucer' brought by William Brazel.

He told UFO researchers Kevin Randle and Donald Schmitt that some strange debris had been brought in while he had been working at the Wright Patterson Air Force Base in 1947. It was lightweight and apparently indestructible. There were also rumours circulating around the base, he said, that bodies had been recovered out of a 'craft from space'.

Another retired air force officer, Brigadier General Thomas Dubose, alleged in interviews that the Roswell Incident had been treated with the greatest secrecy and that the White House had been involved. He also confirmed that the 'weather balloon' story had been fabricated. Other senior ex-officers then emerged with similar tales to tell: they had either seen the bodies of alien creatures who had died when the craft crashed or

they had heard of their existence. Much of this evidence was dismissed by sceptics as second-hand. Yet there remained disturbing anomalies in the government's weather balloon story, so – not surprisingly – questions continued to be asked.

SECRET SURVEILLANCE?

Several theories were advanced. The first, and in the opinion of many people, the most persuasive, was that the debris was surveillance equipment that was being used in a top secret government project designed to spy on Russian nuclear activity, called Mogul. The incident needed to be hushed up because of the clandestine nature of the operation, which is why the army came up with the story about the weather balloon. However, this theory does not explain why the material found on the ranch was so unusual, or why the army would be using such material. It was also pointed out that the army had previously been unconcerned about people

The autopsy exhibit at the UFO Museum in Roswell, New Mexico. After they had retired, several military officers claimed that they saw alien bodies after the incident.

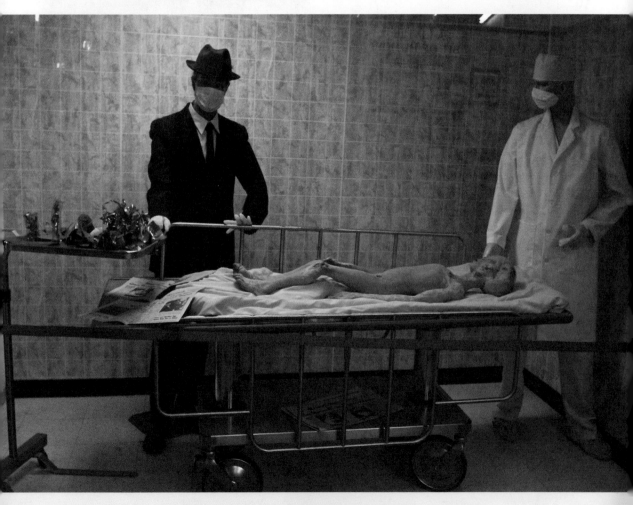

stumbling across the evidence of balloons and other army equipment found scattered in the desert: but this time they rushed to hide it.

Next came the idea that the incident could be attributed to a nuclear accident on the part of the army but, once again, there were problems with this explanation. For a start, the army had no assembled nuclear weapons in its arsenal at the time and there were no other nuclear accidents during the period in question, as public records now attest. Critics also argued that if the army had lost a nuclear weapon in the desert they would surely not have waited for a passing rancher to let them know where it was!

SO WHAT REALLY HAPPENED?

Because of the government secrecy surrounding the issue, a number of UFO researchers have come to the conclusion that some kind of covert activity must have taken place. Some believe that there was an alien landing and that the United States government simply denied the fact in order to prevent panic among the public. Others suggest that the government has access to alien technology but refuses to admit it. There has even been speculation that this was either a crash between two alien spacecraft or a crash involving a spy craft which secretly experimented on live human beings. This latter theory, advanced by Nick Redfern in his book *Body Snatchers in the Desert*, has gained credibility within the UFO field, if not outside it.

Ultimately, it seems that right up to this day nobody really knows what took place. Even the most persuasive theories that have been advanced appear to be full of loose ends. However, whether or not we believe that alien beings landed in the desert that day, what we do know is that there was a lot more to the incident than a burst weather balloon. And that is why, for the foreseeable future, UFO researchers and others will continue to ask: what really happened at Roswell?

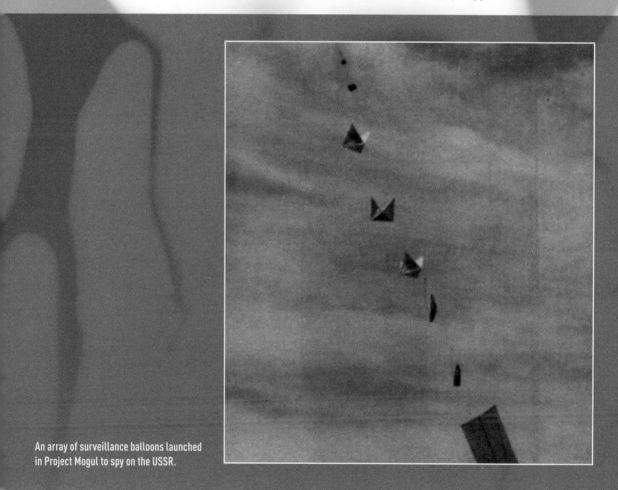

An array of surveillance balloons launched in Project Mogul to spy on the USSR.

In the early hours of Boxing Day, 1980, a strange incident occurred in Rendlesham Forest, Suffolk. Close to the pine forest was an American Air Force Base, which suddenly began to track an unidentified craft on its radar. The base was immediately put on full alert, but after a while it became clear that the craft was not aggressive and that there was no real threat. However, a patrol was sent to the forest to investigate. After the patrol had reached the site by following a dark, narrow path the men saw bright beams of red and blue light shining from what appeared to be a metallic craft that had landed in the forest. Other craft hovered silently in the sky above.

TRANCE-LIKE STATE

Base Commander Gordon Williams reported that he approached the craft on the ground and communicated with the creatures in it through sign language. Other witnesses told of watching the creatures repair their

The dark coniferous trees of Rendlesham Forest.

Locals reported flickering red and blue lights in the trees.

craft, which had become damaged when it crashed in the forest, and then take off in a huge burst of speed and light.

After the craft had left, the airmen said that they had found themselves in a trance-like state so that general confusion prevailed. Local people also reported that their farm animals and domestic pets had become disorientated and panic-stricken, to the extent that they had been running out on to the roads and colliding with vehicles. There were also accounts that flickering blue and red lights played over the trees throughout the rest of the night. Some people even said that small creatures with domed heads had been seen wandering through the forest.

EVIDENCE OF ALIENS

Because of the airmen's confused condition at the time, it was difficult to verify exactly what had happened. However, the indisputable fact was that a very strange occurrence had taken place in the forest, one that could not easily be explained. On the next day, forensic tests were carried out over the whole site and some odd facts emerged.

Firstly, there were some marks on the ground where the landing legs of the craft were thought to have been. These gave out very high levels of radiation. Secondly, the treetops in the area had been damaged as though an aeroplane or other large object had crashed through them. And thirdly, a tape recording of the search had been made by an airman at the time and there were strange noises on it.

To this day, why the radiation levels on the site went up and why the trees in the vicinity were damaged remains a mystery. However, some have disputed the veracity of this tape, claiming that it is a hoax. Since the incident, it has also been rumoured that a video recording of the whole event exists. It was supposedly made by one of the airmen who witnessed it from start to finish. Because this material was so sensitive, it is thought that the military confiscated it and that it then became classified information, never to be made public.

CONSPIRACY THEORY?

Many believe that the hushing up of the incident was a conspiracy by the United States military, who were attempting to cover up the fact that there had been a nuclear accident at Rendlesham. In order to avoid local panic, and to deflect criticism, the personnel at the air base pretended that some kind of alien landing had taken place. Other commentators have put forward the theory that the event was actually an American attack on a Russian spy satellite and that it was the satellite, not an alien craft, that was brought down in the forest.

Various other conspiracy theories have been put forward. It has been suggested that the strange craft were top secret air force aerospace vehicles, known as TR-3Bs or 'Astras'. Inside each of these huge vehicles,

it is said, is a nuclear reactor that negates the Earth's magnetic field, so that the craft becomes very light.

It can then move quickly and flexibly within the magnetic field it has created. In addition to the 'Astras' there are smaller craft with similar capabilities, so the story goes, called TR-3As or 'Black Mantas'.

Critics of this theory have pointed out that it would be very difficult to house a nuclear reactor in this way, because it would be extremely heavy. This has then given rise to another theory, that the United States military is in possession of alien technology.

OTHER SIGHTINGS

There are many other well-documented sightings of 'black triangle' UFOs such as the one that is believed to

have landed at Rendlesham Forest in 1980. Most of these have been seen in and around the coast of the United States, particularly near air force bases. According to reports, the UFOs are hundreds of feet long, they make no sound and they either hover or fly very rapidly. One of the most significant of these sightings was at Ans, in Belgium, where on 30 March 1990 the local citizens reported seeing a hovering black triangle over the city. Members of the Belgian Air Force pursued the craft but were not able to keep up with it. They later issued a report admitting that they could not identify the phenomenon. Similarly, on 13 March 1997 in Phoenix, Arizona, citizens noticed 'black triangle' craft forming a 'V' in the sky. Later, the air force reported that what people had seen were flare tests, but this seemed highly unlikely.

Today, the consensus seems to be that such aircraft do actually exist. The Belgian Air Force has evidence of the 'black triangle' aircraft that visited Ans that day in the shape of radar tracking, photographs and film. What we still do not know, however, is where the craft come from, who they belong to, how they function and why they appear. Could the black triangles, as some suggest, be evidence of top-secret, advanced US military technology? Are they perhaps signs from an underground, possibly terrorist group, who want to display their might in this way? Or could they indeed be visitations from extraterrestrial beings? At present, and for the foreseeable future, the mystery remains.

CROP CIRCLES: ALIEN VISITORS OR LOCAL HOAXERS?

The mysterious appearance of circular patterns in cornfields first hit the headlines during the 1970s, when several of them appeared in England. After these sightings, many people around the world began to report the occurrence of curious, and in some cases very beautiful, patterns in paddy fields and pine forests as well as on snow-covered hills. Critics immediately dismissed the circles as hoaxes and, indeed, some individuals came forward claiming that they had made the circles as a prank.

However, on closer inspection, it became clear that the phenomenon could not be explained so easily. Many aspects of it were very puzzling. For example, the circles typically appeared rapidly; their patterns were complex and very accurate, as though drawn by a compass; and the biological structure of the plants that formed them had changed. Eminent scientists began to conduct research into crop circles and they came up with numerous theories as to how such phenomena could occur. For example, magnetic fields and different types of geological formation could be affecting the plants, causing them to flatten and change.

Yet, to date, no one has come up with a conclusive theory that explains how crop circles have come about. The popular belief that they are evidence of extraterrestrial beings, perhaps messages to humanity from a higher intelligence on a different planet, continues to predominate.

THE FIRST CROP CIRCLES

Within the ancient folklore of Britain and Northern Europe can be found stories of circles in grass or cornfields. They were thought to be caused by elves and fairies and they could cause disaster if people trod on them. A sixteenth-century woodcut shows a picture of a monstrous creature making a circle in a cornfield. However, there are various interpretations of the image and it could well refer to an entirely imaginary event. The first scientific evidence did not appear until the twentieth century, when aerial surveys revealed what were then termed 'crop marks' which were thought to be caused by changes in the soil. Many of the sites were investigated and archaeological finds were made, but little attention was paid to the 'crop marks' themselves.

A crop circle of flattened wheat in Turin, Italy.

FLYING SAUCERS

It was not until 1972 that two men, Arthur Shuttlewood and Bryce Bond, reported seeing a crop circle appear before them on a moonlit night at a place called Star Hill, near Warminster in England. They had come out to look for unidentified flying objects, or UFOs, which had apparently been seen many times in the area over a period of ten years or so. Instead, an imprint on the vegetation suddenly materialized before their eyes, opening up like a fan.

After that, many witnesses from around the world, from Japan to the Soviet Union, came forward with similar stories. Apart from the circles, they also told of having seen aircraft and beams of light and heard a high trilling sound. Reported sightings of crop circles increased in number, until they reached the current figure of over 9,000. There are thought to be many more that go unreported each year.

DOUG AND DAVE

Doug and Dave were pranksters who came forward to announce that they had created the crop circles. They claimed that all of them had been made using planks of wood, string and a baseball cap. However, as more complex patterns were reported it became clear that Doug and Dave could not possibly have made such complicated circles. Moreover, because reports were coming in from all over the world, it was hard to explain how they had been in so many places at the same time. In the end, Doug and Dave had to admit that they were not responsible for all the crop circles that were being reported.

GENUINE FORMATIONS

Once the formations had been looked at scientifically, it began to become clear that human beings could not possibly have made them. When plants from the circles were analyzed under the microscope, it was noticed that their biological structure had changed. Not only this, but nodes on the plant stems appeared to have been blown open in a way that was consistent with them having been heated up. In many cases, otherwise brittle stems were bent but not broken, something that would have been impossible for human beings to do by hand.

Crop circle near the Iron Age burial mound of Silbury Hill in Wiltshire, England. Although there is much anecdotal evidence for the mysterious properties of crop circles, there is very little that is scientifically verifiable.

Another odd aspect of the formations was that they seemed to alter the magnetic field of the area, so that camera crews filming them suddenly discovered that their equipment was not working. Compasses, mobile phones and batteries also stopped working when they were close to the formations. Aircraft flying above them also reported equipment failure. People living in villages that were close to where circles appeared often told of power cuts, cars failing to start and animals refusing to walk across or near the circles.

WHAT CAUSES CIRCLES?

Most people prefer not to believe that little green aliens travelling around the planet in flying saucers are responsible for the happenings, so a variety of other explanations have been sought. Archaeologists, geologists and others have pointed to the fact that crop circles often occur over the Earth's magnetic energy lines, which are also known as ley lines. Early humankind often built structures in these places: Stonehenge is just one example. Recent thinking suggests that eddies in the Earth's magnetic field cause crops to flatten and that other environmental factors, such as underground water tables, may make the nodes of plant stems swell up as if heated.

However, this by no means accounts for the appearance of all crop circles, especially the very complex ones. There remains a great deal of controversy over whether the most spectacular crop circles occur naturally, whether they are the work of human beings or whether they are evidence of alien intervention. It is certainly true that many groups of artists and nature lovers make crop circles, either because they believe that they have a healing effect on the human psyche or because they feel that they are beautiful to look at. However, many have argued that such activity cannot account for every instance of the phenomenon.

Thus, until scientists come up with a completely persuasive explanation for the way in which crop circles suddenly appear on our landscape, enthusiasts will continue to believe that they are the result of supernatural forces. Not little green men, perhaps, but forms of life that, as yet, we know nothing about.

The ancient stone circle of Stonehenge is thought to be erected in a significant position in the Earth's magnetic field; could crop circles be caused by this powerful network of invisible forces?

THE MEN

Do the Men in Black suppress evidence of alien life?

ho are the men in black? Legend has it that these elusive figures are a group of agents that materialize whenever an unidentified flying object appears or any other extraterrestrial occurrence takes place. Their task is to harass or frighten witnesses into denying all knowledge of what has happened. The conspiracy theory that lies behind the idea of the men in black is that alien beings are threatening our planet and want to hide the information from the public. Alternatively, it has been suggested that the men in black are government agents who also wish to suppress the truth.

According to the theory, the government agents or 'MIBs' are usually dressed in black suits and display behaviour which is unusual and, possibly, non-human. They threaten witnesses and confiscate photographs, video tapes and any other means of recording a sighting. In some cases, their black suits have been described as being made of a strange shiny fabric which witnesses have not seen before. They have also been described as 'mechanical', with monotonous voices and robotic movements.

Some reports even attest to the fact that their faces are not like human faces but have odd slanted eyes and high cheekbones. They are said to travel in threes most of the time, but they have occasionally been reported as travelling alone.

MIBs, so the story goes, drive new Lincolns or Cadillacs, often with the headlights off, and the insides of the cars are lit with a strange green or purple light. The licence plates of the cars are false and there are sometimes odd emblems on the doors. Occasionally, the MIBs arrive in black helicopters and tail witnesses of UFO happenings, intimidating them into giving up any evidence they might have.

IN BLACK

FIRST SIGHTINGS

Since the earliest times, there have always been accounts of emissaries from the gods, or from devils, who disguise themselves to do their masters' business on Earth. In particular, demons were said to wear black, usually sporting the fashions of the day, and to ride about in black carriages in a similar way to the Men in Black of today's urban tales. An eighteenth-century Norwegian story tells of a young girl who was travelling with her grandmother to meet the devil (who turned out to be her grandfather!)

The Men in Black drive Lincolns or Cadillacs with the lights off, according to the rumours.

and who, on the way, met three men dressed in black. Another, from the early twentieth century, tells of a religious cult that was centred around a woman named Mary Jones. Its members reported seeing strange lights in the sky and encountering 'dread apparitions' in the night, including men dressed in black.

There has also been speculation among some ufologists that mythical figures from the past, such as Elizabethan and Native American 'black men' or nineteenth-century evil travelling salesmen, could in fact have been 'Men in Black' who were travelling the Earth in order to silence those who had witnessed extraterrestrial events.

The first modern sighting, however, took place in 1947, when a sailor named Harold Dahl reported seeing six unidentified flying objects at a place called Maury Island near Tacoma, Washington. Dahl, who was with his son and his dog, took some photographs. His dog was reportedly killed when some hot sparks from the UFOs landed on the boat. Next day, a man called at his home and took him out to a diner for breakfast. The man, who was tall and dark and wearing a black suit, pumped him for details of the sighting and gave him a severe warning not to tell anyone of it – otherwise his family might be harmed. Later, Dahl claimed that the sighting was a hoax. This was apparently an attempt to follow the MIB's orders, but it caused some confusion and many began to doubt the veracity of his story.

ALBERT K. BENDER

One of the earliest people to pick up on the story was Albert K. Bender, director of the 'International Flying Saucer Bureau' and editor of a UFO newsletter entitled The Space Review. In a 1953 article, Bender alleged that he had acquired information about flying saucers but was unable to print it and warned that anyone who had similar information was in danger. Issues of The Space Review then ceased. Later, Bender explained what had happened. He said that he had been visited by three men in dark suits who had told him the secrets of UFOs and then intimidated him into silence.

After Bender's story was made public, controversy arose around the question of whether or not the 'Men in Black' story had been dreamed up by UFO enthusiasts to cover up the fact that they had very little evidence for their stories. Sceptics pointed out that having government or alien agents harass UFO witnesses into silence was a very handy device for explaining why concrete information was not forthcoming.

Albert K. Bender claimed to have been visited by three mysterious agents in dark suits who forced him to keep quiet about his knowledge of UFOs.

The ufologists, such as writer Gray Barker, Bender's friend, countered by alleging that 'sinister men' were suppressing the real story of what was going on in the extraterrestrial world.

RETURN OF THE MEN IN BLACK

In 1976, a visit from a 'man in black' was reported in Maine, by Dr Herbert Hopkins, who had been told about a UFO sighting in the area. According to Hopkins, the man was dressed in a smart black suit but looked extremely strange, with a pale face and bright red lipstick. He threatened Hopkins in a slow, monotonous voice, telling him not to publicize the UFO encounter in any way. He then walked out, leaving Hopkins in a trance-like state.

Four years later there was another visit, this time to Peter Rojcewicz, a folklorist, while he was in the library at Pennsylvania University. A tall man with a dark face, dressed in a black suit, came up behind him and began to question him about his studies. Rojcewicz told the man that he was researching UFO

Men in Black: Tommy Lee Jones confronts an alien in the film of the same name.

encounters, whereupon the man became angry but then calmed down. After he left, Rojcewicz became panicky and went to find help, but there seemed to be nobody around. Later, he realized that there had been people in the library all along, but he had not been able to see them.

WHO ARE THE MIBS?

According to US government sources, there is some evidence to suggest that people who have witnessed UFO activity have sometimes been harassed. It is thought that ordinary members of the public have sometimes posed as government officials and intimidated witnesses. In one case, witness Rex Heflin of Santa Ana, California, took photographs of a UFO in 1965, which were published. He later told of receiving a visit from two men who claimed to be representatives of the North American Aerospace Defense Command. They asked for the negatives of the photographs and took them away, never to return them.

Although this case was well documented, there were thought to be many inconsistencies in Heflin's account and to date there is little concrete evidence to suggest that the Men in Black actually exist. One complicating factor is that those who claim to have been visited by them often report themselves to have been in a trance-like mental state both during the encounter and after it. This has led some commentators to believe that instead of having been visited by MIBs, the 'witnesses' have actually been undergoing some kind of mental crisis which has impaired their state of mind, so that they imagined the whole event.

Another explanation, advanced by the pro-UFO lobby, is that government officials have in fact dressed up in strange clothes in order to discredit the stories of UFO witnesses. Others suggest that the MIBs are in fact alien-human hybrids whose job it is to cover up any trace of alien activity on Earth. Whatever the truth, it seems that these visits have a long history – whether as real events, or as stories that have moved from the folklore of the past to present-day urban mythology – and they look set to continue in the future.

THE MOON LANDINGS

It is one of the iconic images of the past century: Neil Armstrong emerging from Apollo 11 and uttering the immortal words 'That's one small step for man, one giant leap for mankind' – words so apt that they seemed to have been scripted. But what if the whole thing actually was scripted? What if the moon landings never really happened, but were mocked up in a film studio as a propaganda exercise?

That is precisely the belief of an increasing number of Americans. It is an apparently outlandish conspiracy theory that was ridiculed when it first appeared in the early 1970s but has slowly gained credence ever since. After Watergate, Americans became immeasurably more cynical about their government. So when the 1978 film *Capricorn One* portrayed a NASA attempt to fake a landing on Mars, many were prompted to suspect that the film was actually based on inside information. Since then opinion polls have consistently indicated that millions of Americans have their doubts about the

Walking on the moon: Buzz Aldrin's gold-plated visor mirrored the Eagle landing module and Neil Armstrong, who took most of the pictures.

NASA 69-HC-684

moon landings. These doubts were fanned by a Fox documentary made in 2002, which gave the conspiracy theorists the chance to put their case.

WERE THE LANDINGS FAKED?

So what is that case? What is it about the moon landings, watched by millions at the time and for many years after seen as evidence of one of mankind's supreme achievements, that makes the conspiracy theorists suspicious?

Perhaps the best known questions posed by the conspiracy theorists are to do with the photographs of the landings. Why does the American flag appear to be waving in the wind when the moon has no wind? And why are there no stars visible in the sky? Not only that, why do photographs that purport to be taken miles apart appear to have identical backgrounds?

So what explanations can NASA, or anyone else, offer to explain these apparent anomalies? Well, quite a few. Taking them in order: the flag is apparently waving because it had just been unwrapped and then twisted as the flagpole was screwed into the ground. The reason no

stars are visible is because the cameras that were used were set for quick shutter speeds, in order not to over-expose the film in the very bright light. The dim light of the stars simply does not have a chance to show up on the film. This same effect can easily be observed on Earth. If you take a picture of the night sky with the camera set for a bright sunny day then the stars will be invisible. The allegation that the backgrounds are identical in different photographs does not stand up to detailed analysis either. A careful comparison of the backgrounds that are claimed to be identical in fact shows significant changes in the relative positions of the hills.

It is just the same on Earth, where a mountain range will appear in much the same place in the backgrounds of photographs taken several hundred feet apart.

WHY NO BLAST CRATER?

The photographs are just one set of issues that have been raised by the conspiracy theorists, however. Some of their other questions deal with more mechanical matters.

That the astronaut is brightly lit when he is in the shadow of the lander proves for many people the presence of a second light source – an impossibility on the moon. The effect is, however, caused by the reflection of light from the ground.

Why was there no blast crater visible following the lunar landings? Why did the launch rocket not produce a visible flame? How did the spaceship and its crew survive the journey through the Van Allen radiation belt?

Here are the official scientific responses. There was no blast crater for the simple reason that the Lunar Modules braked before landing, rather than crashing violently into the moon's surface. In any case, their impact was diminished by the much weaker gravity

US geologist and astronaut Harrison Hagan Schmitt takes rock samples from the surface of the moon during America's last lunar landing mission of the twentieth century, Apollo 17, December 1972.

on the moon. There was no visible flame because the Lunar Module used hydrazine and dinitrogen tetroxide, propellants chosen for their ability to ignite upon contact and without a spark. Such propellants happen to produce a nearly transparent exhaust. As for the Van Allen belt, the mission was well prepared for this. The orbital transfer trajectory from Earth to the moon through the belts was selected to minimize radiation exposure so that the spacecraft moved through the belts in just 30 minutes. The astronauts were protected from the radiation by the metal hulls of the spacecraft. The dosage received by the astronauts was no more than that gained from a chest X-ray.

MOON ROCKS

Finally, one particularly complex part of the conspiracy theory has to do with the question of the moon rocks. These are usually seen as the ultimate proof that the moon landings did indeed take place. How else could these rocks, completely different to anything seen on Earth, have come into the possession of NASA? Conspiracy theorists point to the Antarctic expedition of Wernher von Braun, two years prior to the Apollo mission. According to this theory, this mission was used to collect lunar meteorite rocks that could be used as fake moon rocks in a hoax. Von Braun was susceptible to pressure from the authorities. He would have agreed to the conspiracy in order to protect himself from recriminations over his past as a former Nazi.

Well it is a nice theory and it does have some scientific rationale. There are indeed lunar meteorites to be found in Antarctica. However, the first meteorite identified as a lunar meteorite was not found until 1981, over a decade after the moon landings. It was only identified as such because of its similarity to the lunar samples returned by Apollo, which in turn are similar to the few grams of material returned from the moon by Soviet sample return. The total collection of identified Antarctic lunar meteorites presently amounts to only about 2.5 kg (5.5 lb), less than one per cent of the 381 kg (840 lb) of moon rocks and soil returned by Apollo. Furthermore, the detailed analysis of the lunar rocks by many different scientists around the world shows no evidence of their having been on Earth prior to their return.

For every point raised by the conspiracy theorists there seems to be a rational scientific explanation. So is there any likelihood that America faked the moon landings? Not really. As scientists have pointed out, given the amount of work it would have taken to fool the world on such an epic scale it would have been easier to just go to the moon.

AREA 51 AND UFO DISCLOSURE

No government facility has as much of an imprint in conspiracy culture as the one commonly known as Area 51. A mysterious, sprawling compound in the foreboding flats of the Nevada desert, Area 51 is where some of America's most advanced aircraft have supposedly been tested.

Those who work there can't discuss what they do, and those who try to get in are greeted with threats that they will be shot on sight. Beyond that, some conspiracy theorists believe it to be a place where alien ships are back-engineered, powerful weapons developed and aliens themselves tested on. If it wasn't, they reason, why is there so much mystery surrounding the place? Why don't we know anything about what's happening now and what's been done there in the past? And why, to this day, are alien-looking craft spotted flying there?

But while Area 51 was indeed once shrouded in mystery, recent intelligence disclosures have taken much of the intrigue away from the place. Area 51, which is never actually called that by the people who work there, is still a classified test facility doing things that the general public will likely never find out about. But thanks to declassification and former employees being allowed to tell their stories, we know a great deal about the place's past – and how the work done there has changed aviation history.

SECRET WEAPONS AT A SECRET PLACE

Like so many other subjects, conspiracy theories about Area 51 caught on because it's a real place – surrounded by real secrecy. While the US Air Force generally doesn't acknowledge its existence, the fact that it does exist has been common knowledge for three decades. Yet everything that happens there is classified at the highest level – Top Secret/Sensitive Compartmented Information.

This puts Area 51 into a hazy area: a real place that spends tax dollars on projects that taxpayers aren't allowed to know anything about. This secrecy wasn't always baked into the facility, however. In its earliest incarnation, the dry bed at Groom Lake, Nevada, was simply a pair of unpaved runways used during World War II, and given the un-mysterious name Indian Springs Air Force Auxiliary Field.

In the early 1950s, the Atomic Energy Commission was looking for places to set off nuclear bomb tests, so they bought up a huge tract of desert, called it the Nevada Test Site, and parcelled it into numbered Areas. A few years later, the CIA needed a place to test a high-flying spy plane codenamed AQUATONE. The flat land of Groom Lake was perfect, and so an unused part of the Nevada Test Site was designated as Area 51, and became the location where AQUATONE was put through its paces.

Over the next few decades, the tract of land expanded to include about 1,000 employees – many flown in from Las Vegas or Los Angeles on secretive, unmarked flights. AQUATONE gave way to an even faster reconnaissance plane known as OXCART, and Area 51 also became the destination of choice to test captured Soviet fighter planes, as well as the testing

Area 51 is still a restricted site, a fact pointed out by conspiracy theorists who believe the government has something to hide.

Groom Lake in the Nevada Desert is the location of Area 51, an American government facility shrouded in mystery.

involvement in a 10,000-year pact with a civilization from the Zeta Reticuli star system, and about forms of physics and engineering that were centuries ahead of our own technology. He claimed to have taken part in test flights of nine different alien craft, and been involved in the explosion of an alien element.

of two alien-looking stealth planes known as HAVE BLUE and TACIT BLUE.

None of this was public at the time, of course. In fact, Area 51 had no real public imprint until 1989, when a man going only by the name 'Dennis' told a Las Vegas TV reporter a fantastical tale of alien ships, fantastical-looking craft and secrets of the highest nature. 'Dennis' claimed to be an engineer at a classified testing facility called S-4, located near Area 51. 'Dennis' worked in a hangar built into a mountainside, back-engineering a disc-shaped alien spacecraft to reveal its secrets: anti-gravity propulsion, the ability to change directions on a dime, invisibility and incredible power driven by an undiscovered element. 'Dennis' learned about Earth's

Within a few years, the conspiracy theory about Area 51 had grown to encompass the cold storage of alien bodies taken from the Roswell crash, faked moon landings, mutated Soviet midget pilots, weather control mechanisms, directed energy weapons, and tunnels to secret underground bases which were all alleged elements of the 'real story' of Area 51.

And these stories were augmented by countless UFO sightings of strangely shaped aircraft doing strange things in the sky over Area 51, not to mention the unmarked planes carrying employees and the total silence from anyone in the government about all of it. The CIA even forbade NASA from publishing an image taken via satellite of the Groom Lake area in 1974 – an event revealed in a memo declassified in

A photo of the military base at Area 51 taken in 1996.

The HAVE BLUE project was a prototype for the F-117 stealth plane. This plane was a good match for the descriptions of UFOs seen over Nevada.

2006 that called Groom Lake 'the most sensitive spot' on Earth.

The goings-on at Area 51 are just one part of a supposed 'secret space programme', theorized by conspiracy believers as a parallel NASA, using alien and back-engineered Nazi technology to build giant bases on the moon, anti-gravity spacecraft, powerful energy weapons, and even study the rudiments of time travel and light speed.

And it's still happening. In February 2018, two amateur UFO spotters made national news when they captured footage of two F-16 fighters appearing to dogfight a triangular craft jumping around in the sky. Naturally, the air force had no comment.

THE SECRECY FALLS AWAY

Much of what happens at Area 51 is still classified, but the bloom of secrecy has decidedly gone off the facility. The government made its first declassification of Area 51 documents in 1991. That's when long-time UFO watchers were mildly disappointed to learn that AQUATONE was actually the U-2 spy plane, OXCART was the codename for the SR-71 spy plane, and HAVE BLUE was an early concept version of the F-117 stealth fighter. This oddly shaped plane fits perfectly with the description of the craft seen flitting about the Nevada skies.

In 2007, many former Area 51 employees had their confidentiality agreements lifted. Cold War-era workers who'd been silent for nearly 50 years told incredible stories of working on deeply classified projects, being paid in cash or by non-existent front companies, scaring off local deputies who arrived at sites where secret planes crashed, and, oddly enough, how great the food was. They were proud of the work they'd done, and reunions of former Area 51 employees were common – though always secret. And there was even more disclosure of classified information in 2013, when the CIA officially acknowledged its existence thanks to a Freedom of Information lawsuit. What none of these reports contained were long-held secrets about aliens, anti-gravity, faked moon landings, or UFOs. There weren't any. 'Dennis', who first put the idea of aliens at Area 51 in popular culture, turned out to be a UFO enthusiast named Bob Lazar who never attended

A map of the Nevada test range around Groom Lake, where Area 51 is located. The veil of secrecy around the area is slowly being lifted, and now even Google Maps shows the airstrips at the base.

any of the advanced schools he claimed to have, and likely spent very little time at Groom Lake – yet still clings to his stories of fantastical technology and alien experimentation.

What really happens there now is still classified, of course. Radio traffic there is still coded to mask the names and types of planes flying in and out, and snoopers who find ways to evade security will likely learn little and quickly be sent away. But while the secrecy is still there, the idea of Groom Lake being 'the most sensitive spot on Earth' is falling away. Google Maps includes outlines of the airstrips at Groom Lake, the 'triangular craft' seen dogfighting F-16s in 2018 was quickly revealed to be a bird, and the Air Force is even posting job ads for pilots to ferry staff from Las Vegas' McCarron Airport to the base. But the planes they'd be flying are still unmarked.

NIBIRU/PLANET X

Stories of great space cataclysms are a staple of both literature and science. Some of it is good old fashioned folklore, passed down through the generations. And some is scientifically accurate work that's been studied for decades, such as the generally accepted theory that a massive asteroid impact in the Yucatan caused the mass extinction that wiped out the dinosaurs. But there are also a number of people who have seized on the alluring idea of a hidden planet or asteroid lurking out there in the darkness to advance their own conspiracy theories, sell books, or set themselves up as modern-day prophets.

The 'Nibiru' conspiracy theory falls squarely into that last category. Every few years, tabloid articles and pseudoscientific prophecies seem to hail the coming of a planet-sized object in a distant orbit that will impact Earth at a time only they know for sure – a time that never seems to arrive. While Nibiru, the name often given to that object, is a different concept from that of 'Planet X', the two are often lumped together and used as interchangeable terms. One is an actual scientific theory that has been proposed by great minds in astronomy, and meticulously studied over the span of decades. The other is a fantastical concept of a woman who claimed to have been experimented upon by aliens, working from a book written by a supposed scientist and linguist who actually had no background in either. Determining the differences between the two is a useful way to practise scientific scepticism, as well as to introduce critical thinking concepts into a story that often gets hyped far beyond its importance.

THE STORY OF NIBIRU

The idea of a large, undiscovered planet lurking beyond eighth planet Neptune has fascinated astronomers for over a century. In fact, even before Neptune was discovered in 1846, scientists believed a massive object must be responsible for the irregularities in the orbit of seventh planet Uranus. They saw deviations in its trajectory that seemingly only could have been caused by the gravity of something extremely large and close. In 1906, American astronomer Percival Lowell began searching the skies for an object he called 'Planet X', with the X signifying 'unknown' rather than the number ten, as Pluto hadn't been discovered. Lowell's search, along with the investigation of a number of other astronomers, proved fruitless, even after Pluto was found, as the former planet wasn't big enough to be the source of Uranus' anomalous orbit. No other trans-Neptunian object was ever found that would fit the description needed.

It's very common for pseudoscience to attempt to explain something that science can't. So it shouldn't be surprising that a series of cranks, fake prophets, and others rushed into the void left by the non-discovery of Planet X. In the mid-1970s, when it was becoming clear that Pluto wasn't the large object past Neptune that had been hoped for, an author and pseudohistorical scholar named Zecharia Sitchin made up his own explanation. His 1976 book *The 12th Planet* posited a massive planetoid depicted in Sumerian mythology as the cause of a number of mass extinctions on Earth, and gave it the name 'Nibiru' based on his own translation of an unknown word found on a cuneiform tablet. At no point has any reputable scientist or astronomer confirmed that Sitchin's Nibiru is real, and if it actually did exist, it would be so disruptive to the orbits of the actual planets that the solar system would essentially fly apart. It would also be easily seen in the night sky. Beyond that, Sitchin's grasp of the Sumerian language was rudimentary, and it's likely that he mistranslated the tablet he was working with.

But none of those objections made any difference to Sitchin's growing fanbase, who readily bought a seemingly endless series of books about the secret goings-on in history and astronomy. One of Sitchin's most vocal fans was a woman named Nancy Lieder, a self-described psychic and telepath, who claimed to have been kidnapped and experimented upon as a child by aliens from Zeta Reticuli (also the home of David Icke's reptoid-fighting grey aliens (see page 96)). Lieder had started the website ZetaTalk in 1995, as an early hub of discussion about aliens, UFOs, and conspiracy theories. Around that time, as the Hale-Bopp comet was approaching its closest distance to Earth, Lieder put forth a shocking theory on ZetaTalk: that Hale-

Bopp was actually being used as a diversion from the real threat to Earth, which was the 12th planet, making its once-every-3,400-years approach.

'Hale-Bopp is nothing more than a distant star, and will draw no closer,' Lieder wrote on the site on 6 August 1995. 'The 12th Planet, a true messenger of death, will not even get the attention the fraudulent Hale-Bopp is getting today. That's because it's a real threat, not a diversion.' This was the first of dozens of posts she made about the 'Hale-Bopp Fraud' she felt was being pulled

The astronomer Percival Lowell (1855–1916) began searching for the mysterious 'Planet X' in 1906.

on us by NASA and the scientific establishment, who would do anything to keep the people from learning the truth for fear of panic. The theory caught on with the conspiracy theory media of the time, making Lieder a radio star, and raising her profile to the point that when she declared that Nibiru would hit the Earth around 15 May 2003, it made mainstream news.

2003 – OR 2012 – OR 2017

The day 15 May 2003 came and went without the cataclysm Nancy Lieder had spent almost a decade predicting. Rather than abandon the 'Nibiru' conspiracy theory, she doubled down, saying the date she'd thrown out was merely a bit of disinformation 'designed to fool the establishment'. She then claimed that only she knew the real end-of-days date (thanks to the Zetans who continued to communicate with her), and that giving out the real date would only allow the establishment to keep citizens from fleeing to safety. As with most other conspiracy gurus, Lieder gave out a torrent of implausible and unverifiable claims to bolster her writing, giving it the appearance of profundity.

Regardless, Nibiru was sucked into the frenzy of conspiracy theories and mythology surrounding the Mayan calendar/2012 phenomenon. Despite Mayan and Sumerian mythology being completely different, Nibiru fits well into the hazy beliefs of people who thought the world was ending simply because people

The conspiracy theorist Nancy Lieder argued that the Hale-Bopp comet, which passed by Earth in 1995, was being used as a distraction from the real danger of the 12th planet.

Conspiracy theorists merged beliefs about Nibiru with the supposed predictions of the Mayan calendar that the world would end on 21 December.

they trusted told them so (and the establishment didn't). Again, continuing what conspiracy theorists thought was a massive cover-up, NASA and the science establishment swore up and down that Nibiru wasn't real, and that there was no actual Mayan prophecy about anything happening on 21 December 2012. And they were right, as the 2012 phenomenon was a bust as well. It came back again in 2017, when a fringe astrologer and 'prophet' named David Meade threw out 23 September 2017 as the date that the Bible and an alignment of stars foretold of Nibiru crossing Earth's path. It didn't, so Meade threw out more dates in 2017, then again for 23 April 2018. They all came and went. Meanwhile, evidence that Nibiru or Sitchin's '12th

planet' exist continues to be elusive, kept from us not by a conspiracy but by basic science.

We still don't know the source of the gravitational irregularities in Uranus' orbit, though they likely are caused by a long-ago impact pushing the planet on to its side and having its axis point almost directly at the sun. And scientists continue to scan the skies for objects either past Neptune, or whose orbits take them close to Earth. But the constant drumbeat of prophecies and conspiracies regarding a massive planet that only a few rogue scholars know about has nothing to do with this real scientific research – and everything to do with making money out of the scientifically illiterate.

CHAPTER 6

COVER-UPS

What happens when the string-pullers need to make sure the rest of us don't find out about something terrible they did? They cover it up! And yet, they dot it so badly and sloppily that we find out about it anyway, usually with just a bit of internet searching. From crashed planes that were 'really' hit by missiles to secret government experiments to the real shape of the Earth, here are the conspiracy theories about what the powers that be have been keeping from you.

THE WACO

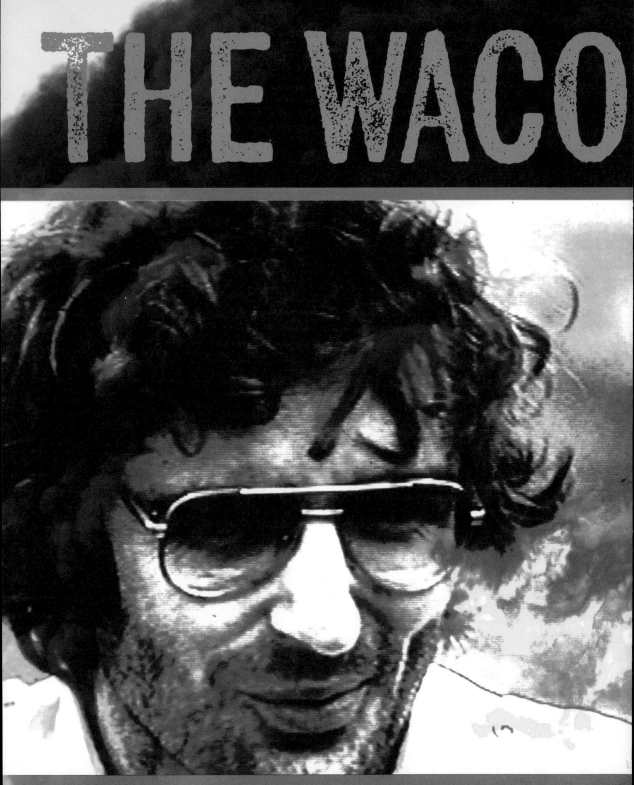

David Koresh, Waco Cult Leader, 1993.

INCIDENT

Over the past 20 years several events have shaken America and made a significant minority of Americans deeply cynical about the behaviour of their own government. Among the most significant of these is the incident that took place at the Branch Davidian compound near Waco, Texas, in early 1993. This culminated in the loss of more than 90 lives as the government appeared to declare war on a tiny religious sect.

The sect in question, the Branch Davidians, were an offshoot of an offshoot of the Seventh Day Adventist Movement. They had been based in a compound called Mount Carmel, outside Waco since the 1930s. By 1955 the leadership of the group had passed to one Benjamin Roden, who was succeeded in time by his wife Lois. In 1981 a charismatic young man named Vernon Howell joined the group and he soon became a leading light, especially after he began an affair with the much older Lois. A power struggle began between Howell and Lois's son George. George Roden was the initial victor and Howell left the group to start his own splinter group in 1984. Lois died in 1986 and George Roden assumed control for two years until Vernon Howell returned and managed to wrest control back from the increasingly mentally unstable George.

Vernon Howell began to impose his own vision on the sect. He decided that he was a Messiah figure and should be allowed to be polygamous. He was believed to have recruited as many as 12 women as his concubines, some of them the wives of other members and some of them as young as 12 years old. As the Messiah he also exempted himself from the sect's restriction on diet and alcohol. In 1990 he gave himself a new, rather more biblical-sounding, name: David Koresh. His teachings became increasingly apocalyptic with the United States government being denounced continually as Babylonians. The compound was renamed Ranch Apocalypse. The group stockpiled enough food to last for a year as well as large quantities

of arms and ammunition. Dealing in guns – legally – also became a significant source of income for the group.

Gradually the activities of the Branch Davidians and their leader started to worry their Texan neighbours. Reports began to appear in the newspapers that Koresh had been accused of abusing children. The Bureau of Alcohol, Tobacco and Firearms started taking an interest in their group. When a postman reported a delivery of what appeared to be grenade casings, the investigation intensified and the bureau found evidence of several minor firearms violations.

Rather than simply waiting for Koresh to make one of his regular visits to the city, however, the BATF decided to launch a huge raid on the compound. Scheduled for 28 February 1993 it was meant to be a surprise but news crews had been tipped off and the BATF helicopter flying over the compound shortly beforehand must have warned the residents that something was amiss.

FORCED TO RETREAT

The agents approached the compound that Sunday morning in vehicles disguised as cattle trailers. However, the Branch Davidians were not fooled and the situation very quickly got out of control. As the agents approached the compound, shots rang out. It is still not clear who fired first, with both sides accusing the other, but before long a full-scale gun battle had broken out. By the time the shooting ended four BATF agents and five Branch Davidians were dead and many more were injured.

The BATF had been forced to retreat because they had underestimated the firepower and determination of the sect members. The raid had been an unqualified disaster which had been caught on film for the world to see. Still, the government could not back down now, so a siege began immediately, with the FBI soon taking over the leadership from the BATF.

The siege lasted for 51 days. During that time the FBI seemed to employ two distinct tactics. On the one hand, hostage negotiators talked regularly with David Koresh and in the early days of the siege they secured the release of several groups of members, mostly children.

However, although the negotiators were accustomed to hostage situations this one was very different. The remaining people inside the compound did not see themselves as hostages. They were determined to stay with their leader and it became increasingly clear that Koresh was not intending to leave in the near future. At the same time, hostile tactics were also being used. After a while, the electricity was cut off to the compound and later on giant floodlights were trained on the building in order to prevent the occupants from sleeping.

Notoriously, the FBI also played tapes at deafening volume to demoralize the occupants – the sounds on the tapes included Tibetan Buddhist chants, bagpipes, seagulls crying, helicopters, dentists' drills, sirens, dying rabbits, a train and songs by Alice Cooper and Nancy Sinatra. Such tactics had been seen to be useful in the operation against the Panamanian leader General Noriega a couple of years before, but the Branch Davidians seemed to be made of sterner stuff and the FBI started to run out of patience. The operation was enormously expensive and the eyes of the world were upon it. Surely the might of the American government could not be halted by a handful of religious fanatics?

UP IN FLAMES

Eventually, Attorney General Janet Reno approved plans for a final assault. This was launched on the morning of Monday 19 April. The FBI called the compound to warn the occupants that they would be using tear gas. Armed vehicles then approached the compound, punched holes in the walls and sprayed tear gas into the building. Still the Davidians refused to leave. Instead, they started firing at the vehicles. Then the telephone was thrown out, a sign that the talking was over. Later, towards noon, as the FBI pondered its next move, the compound went up in flames. Fires were raging and these were soon punctuated by huge explosions. Finally, nine occupants emerged. One woman came out with her clothing in flames and then tried to go back in, but she was restrained by a BATF agent and taken to safety.

It was too dangerous for firefighters to approach the blaze. Even when it appeared to be in its last stages a soldier was shot at when he approached the building. Eventually, however, the compound was razed to the

BATF agents enter a building on the compound through a window.

Explosions rock the Branch Davidian compound as the FBI and BATF begin their assault.

ground and the FBI was able to inspect the damage. They found 80 dead bodies amongst the rubble of which 23 were children (14 of whom were fathered by Koresh). The body of Koresh himself was identified by his dental records. He had been shot in the head.

This was an operation that had gone about as wrong as it possibly could. The FBI tried to stress that the Branch Davidians had set the fires themselves and so had committed mass suicide, but it was inevitable that the conspiracy theorists would soon get to work.

DELIBERATE MURDER?

Essentially the conspiracy theorists were all saying the same thing, that the FBI had deliberately murdered the Branch Davidians. Evidence for this, however, was at first slight but the dogged investigations of a right-wing maverick named Michael McNulty started to raise embarrassing questions. He would air his findings in two successful films about the affair – the Academy Award-nominated *Waco: The Rules of Engagement* and *Waco: A New Revelation*.

Two key allegations are made by McNulty. The first is that the FBI caused the fires. After the event, the FBI had always maintained that it had not used any flammable substance or weapon in its assault on the compound. McNulty discovered, however, that flammable tear gas canisters had been used in the attack. The FBI finally reversed its earlier statements and admitted this in 1999. Secondly, McNulty examined heat-sensitive film of the operation and noticed flashes coming from behind the building. These, he claimed, were muzzle flashes – proof that the FBI had been firing on anyone trying to escape the fire.

Some of McNulty's other charges were supported by rather less documentary evidence. They included the suggestion that soldiers from the army's super-secret Delta Force participated in the attack; that hand-held grenade launchers were fired at the kitchen and could have ignited the fire; and that a demolition charge was placed on the roof of the bunker which was detonated by remote control.

So how has the FBI responded to these charges? The explosion in the bunker has been blamed on the

The aftermath of the siege: the compound is now a burnt-out shell, and over eighty people lie dead in and around its confines.

quantity of arms possessed by the occupants. The use of grenade launchers and the active involvement of Delta Force soldiers (though they were acknowledged to have been present) were both flatly denied. The flashes on the heat-resistant film were written off as reflected sunlight, with experts pointing out that a muzzle would have to be attached to a human being who would also show up on heat-resistant film. As for the flammable CS gas canisters, the FBI says that they were launched four hours prior to the fire breaking out but, in any case, they had failed to reach their target. This was backed up by a civil jury, Congress, the court and the Special Counsel who, in the year 2000, all concluded that the FBI had not caused the fire. The FBI also point out they had introduced bugging devices into the compound which clearly recorded cult members spreading fuel about and preparing to light it.

TRAGIC CONSEQUENCES

All this, of course, has cut little ice with conspiracy theorists. What they and many other Americans point

out was that here was a religious group surrounded by government forces but still going up in flames. The Waco incident made for potent TV images and proved a powerful recruiting aid for the far-right militias.

This incident would bear terrible fruit two years later when, on the anniversary of the Waco deaths, a young man named Timothy McVeigh decided to take vengeance on the government by perpetrating the Oklahoma City bombing.

So, do the conspiracists have a point? Could Waco have been a massive plot by the government against its own people? It seems unlikely, because in the final analysis there is no reason why the government would have actively wanted to bring about the annihilation of this obscure religious cult. What seems far more likely is that this was simply a disastrously badly handled affair. It was less a conspiracy than a shambles. Unfortunately, however, the consequences of the government's actions were tragic, both in the short and the long term.

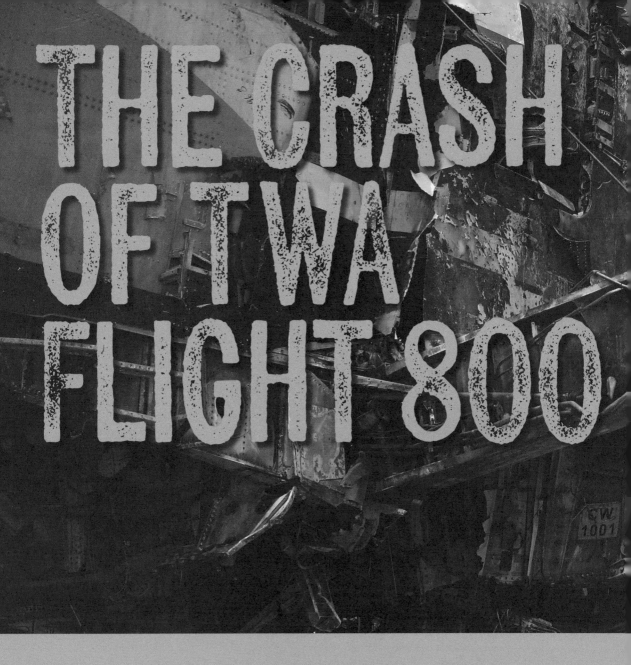

THE CRASH OF TWA FLIGHT 800

Late in the evening on 17 July 1996, TWA Flight 800 took off from New York's John F. Kennedy Airport on a transatlantic flight to Paris. But just 12 minutes into the journey, the plane suffered an explosion, and crashed into the Atlantic Ocean off the coast of Long Island. There were 230 passengers and crew on board, and none survived.

The sheer loss of life and the rarity of major aviation accidents in the United States, along with the nascent internet conspiracy theory movement, combined to create what was maybe the first large-scale online conspiracy theory related to a plane crash. Such theories

are almost a foregone conclusion now, with virtually every major air disaster run through a grinder of false flag allegations, wild theories and connections between minor events. But in 1996, culture in general, and fringe culture in particular, moved much slower. So when a plane full of people simply disappeared, and was the subject of a massive investigation, it naturally led to allegations that the government was lying about what really happened.

The possibility that the plane was shot down by the government, either accidentally or on purpose, became so hotly debated that the government itself carried out tests to disprove it. But did they?

The reconstructed wreckage of the plane from TWA Flight 800. Almost the entire plane was recovered.

A DOOMED FLIGHT, AN INSTANT CONSPIRACY

The location of the crash caused the National Transportation Safety Board's investigation to take much longer than a normal plane crash might. To the NTSB's credit, they managed to recover all of the 230 bodies in ten months, and reassemble 95 per cent of the plane's frame, with the missing pieces deemed too small to be of significance.

But even as debris was painstakingly being moved from the ocean floor to a hangar in upstate New York, a parallel narrative was building: that witnesses saw an 'ascending streak of light' moving towards a part of the sky where a large fireball appeared. The FBI interviewed over 750 witnesses, and over 250 described variations on the same thing: a bright object spiralling, ascending, or streaking towards an aeroplane, followed by an explosion, with the sound following closely behind, and the target falling into the ocean in two pieces. In fact, 38 described such a streak ascending vertically, almost straight up – exactly like a missile would.

The FBI then contracted the CIA to use summaries of this eyewitness testimony (the interviews weren't recorded) to create an animation of what the witnesses

An eyewitness to the explosion answers questions about what happened. Many witnesses described an 'ascending streak of light', implying that a missile had been fired.

Two members of the NTSB take out the voice recorder and flight data recorder from TWA Flight 800. These revealed a normal take-off but failed to reveal the cause of the explosion.

described. And that testimony and animation, along with the involvement of America's most shadowy intelligence agencies and the slow pace of the NTSB investigation, led observers to come to one conclusion: Flight 800 was shot down by a missile.

These theories burbled for years, until the NTSB released its final report in August 2000. The government agency found that Flight 800 was split in two by the explosion of flammable fuel vapours in the plane's centre fuel tank, probably caused by a short circuit in faulty wiring. The explosion sent the two large pieces descending into the ocean, where both shattered.

While the centre fuel tank explosion theory was plausible, the NTSB paid heed to the conspiracy theories. They ran a variety of tests on what witnesses would have seen if a missile had shot the plane down, and deduced that the eyewitness testimony was mistaken. They even tested what it would look like if a missile exploded near the plane, as well as testing what a bomb explosion would do to the plane's frame.

But while the missile theory was disregarded by the report, it resulted in two more nagging questions: why did the plane have 196 tiny impact points on its frame? And why were there trace amounts of explosive residue detected on three samples of material from the recovered aeroplane wreckage? Such impacts and residue would be consistent with the shrapnel caused by a missile exploding next to the plane. And wouldn't the NTSB, an arm of the government, have the motive to cover up the destruction of a passenger plane? If the government shot the plane down accidentally, it would be a scandal of epic proportions. And if it was brought

down by terrorism, it would mean every passenger plane in the world was vulnerable to the forces of evil – possibly bringing down the entire airline industry.

CONSPIRACY THEORIES CAN'T CHANGE THE LAWS OF PHYSICS

So who fired the missile? Why? And how did it happen? Such a missile would have to have been fired from something, either another aeroplane, a land-based instillation, or a boat. Was there anything in the area that could have launched it?

The US military reported that the only aircraft in the area of Flight 800 were a P-3 Orion anti-submarine plane, an HC-130P air-sea rescue support plane and an HH-60G rescue helicopter. While an Orion can theoretically carry air-to-air missiles, they would have no particular reason to be armed with such weapons during peacetime. The other craft don't have the capability to shoot another plane down. The only American naval vessel within eight hours of the area was the Coast Guard Cutter USS *Adak*, armed with only small calibre guns. The *Adak*'s crew won the Coast Guard Unit Commendation for their search and rescue work in the aftermath. If the *Adak* had shot down the plane (with weapons it doesn't carry), would it return to the scene of the crime? After that, there was only the cruiser USS *Normandy*, located almost 300 kilometres south of where Flight 800 exploded – far out of range of anti-aircraft missiles.

Without resorting to making up 'stealth' assets or secret weapons, the next possibility for a missile would be a land-based installation, but there are none in the area of the crash armed with surface-to-air missiles.

A P-3 Orion anti-submarine plane was the only aircraft in the area of the doomed flight. It is unlikely that it would have been carrying air-to-air missiles.

And while some conspiracy theories have pointed to either a shoulder-fired or submarine-fired missile, no man-portable anti-aircraft missile has anywhere near the range needed to have shot down Flight 800. And submarine-launched anti-aircraft missiles have never been deployed in the US Navy due to their inaccuracy.

Any other unknown asset would need to have been scrubbed from the records of every military and civilian radar in the area, with everyone able to report on such an asset eliminated. It would also require all evidence of a fired missile being eliminated, and the faking of a four-year NTSB investigation. Hundreds or even thousands of people would need to be involved, multiple murders would have to be carried out and reams of evidence would have to be destroyed. It would be a cover-up of massive proportions.

Paradoxically, it would also have left seemingly hundreds of witnesses, whose testimony was eventually released publicly. It affirmed that what most saw was consistent with two large, flaming pieces of an aeroplane streaking towards the water. Other testimonies claim to have simultaneously seen and heard the streak and explosion – violating the laws of physics, as the light of the explosion would have been visible about a minute before the sound drew the ears of the witnesses.

As for the minor impact holes? They were likely caused by debris hitting the plane after the explosion. And the explosive residue probably wasn't on the plane initially, as contact with the water would have diluted it. Instead, it was likely the result of the boots of military personnel contacting the wreckage.

In 1996, the internet was ripe for an anti-government conspiracy theory taking off. Flight 800 was the perfect mix of unusual events, government involvement and tragedy. But nothing in the intervening years has changed the NTSB's findings: an internal explosion caused by fuel fumes sparking. It was a once in a decade tragedy, with no satisfactory explanation other than bad luck.

The USS *Adak* responded quickly to the disaster and played a major role in the search and rescue efforts, but that has not stopped conspiracy theorists from suspecting the vessel of foul play.

1333   U.S. COAST GUARD

MIND CONTROL: MKULTRA

A powerful hallucinogen, LSD, was given to subjects of the MKULTRA programme for prolonged periods, sometimes causing permanent mental damage.

L S D

One of the most bizarre and disturbing conspiracies of all time was Project MKULTRA. This was the secret name for a series of CIA experiments that took place from the 1950s to the 1970s, which were designed to explore the possibilities of mind control through the use of drugs such as LSD and mescaline. In these experiments, subjects were given mind-altering drugs, often without their prior knowledge, and their subsequent behaviour was then studied.

In several cases the experiments resulted in the death of one or another of the participants and there were many instances of severe, permanently damaging mental illness. However, the CIA continued to conduct the trials until the project was finally exposed. Ultimately, very little useful information about mind control resulted from MKULTRA and it seems that sadism, rather than serious scientific enquiry, was the driving force behind some of the experiments.

TRUTH DRUGS

MKULTRA was set up by Allen Dulles, head of the CIA, in 1953, in order to look into the use of mind control techniques. The project was led by Dr Sidney Gottlieb, and early research was directed towards trying to find a 'truth drug' for use in the interrogation of Russian spies. The project was wide reaching, with over a hundred research programmes, many of which were secret, and experiments were conducted on army and other personnel without their knowledge.

In the initial phase of the project, the effect of radiation on the human mind was the main focus of research but, as time went on, interest began to centre on the effect of psychotropic drugs, particularly LSD. As the programmes proliferated, subjects began to be recruited from outside the army and the CIA. Patients with mental illnesses (many of them with minor disorders such as mild depression and anxiety),

Head of the CIA Allen Dulles set up the MKULTRA project in 1953.

prostitutes and other types of individual were often used as guinea pigs. An undeniable element of torture crept into the experiments, as Gottlieb began to tie his victims up in straitjackets after administering the drugs. They were often locked in rooms where they could see or hear nothing or tape loops were played to them in an attempt to drive them mad. Gottlieb also ordered his subjects to be given enormous amounts of LSD – in one experiment, volunteers were given the drug for a period of over two months, causing many of them to suffer permanent mental damage.

OPERATION MIDNIGHT CLIMAX

As time went on, the MKULTRA research programmes became ever more bizarre and unpleasant, but they yielded very little in the way of scientific results. One of the most infamous of the experiments was Operation Midnight Climax, in which Dr George Hunter White recruited prostitutes from San Francisco. The prostitutes were asked to administer LSD to their clients without the clients' knowledge. The LSD was put into the victims' drinks and CIA operatives monitored their behaviour through two-way mirrors. No scientific benefits at all accrued from this experiment – the operatives were not trained scientists – and one can only assume that it was set up as a means of satisfying the prurient interests of those who devised it. However, it took more than a decade for this programme to end.

It was later revealed that Dr Gottlieb's behaviour as head of MKULTRA was also questionable. He was known to take large amounts of LSD himself and he seemed obsessed with the drug, even though it began to emerge that it was of very little use as a mind control device. Subjects under the influence of the drug behaved erratically and, if anything, became less susceptible to interrogation than they had been without the drug.

DANGEROUS TREATMENTS

Undeterred by the fact that LSD seemed to be useless as a mind-controlling substance, the MKULTRA team went on to perform more and more dangerous experiments on their hapless victims. In some cases, they simultaneously drip-fed a mixture of amphetamines and barbiturates into their subjects, which resulted in extreme mental confusion and sometimes even death. In addition to the use of LSD, amphetamines and barbiturates, the MKULTRA team experimented with other drugs such as heroin, mescaline, marijuana and alcohol.

Perhaps the worst abuses of all took place in Canada, under the aegis of Dr Ewan Cameron. Dr Cameron had put forward a theory of 'psychic driving' in which he claimed that the mind could be erased and then corrected through drugs and other therapies. He conducted experiments in Montreal over a period of almost a decade, using a combination of electroconvulsive therapy and drugs, both administered at well above the normal levels. He regularly induced comas in his subjects, sometimes for months on end, while playing them tape loops, supposedly to correct their thinking. Not surprisingly, by the end of his treatment, many of his patients were mentally scarred for life.

BLOWING THE WHISTLE

It was not until 1974 that the project came under press scrutiny, when an article in *The New York Times* reported on the CIA's history of experimentation on human beings for the purposes of 'mind control' research. Several committees were set up to look into what had happened, but they found that much of the evidence had gone missing. Many of MKULTRA's records had been destroyed in order to prevent the truth from ever coming out. Even so, there was enough information to show that the MKULTRA project had been very extensive. Over 30 universities and other institutions had been involved and many of the subjects had been completely unaware that they were being given drugs. Not only this, but the experiments were mostly completely pointless from a scientific point of view.

It was also revealed that an army scientist, Frank Olsen, had been given LSD without his knowledge as part of an experiment and had later thrown himself out of a window and died. His family later alleged that he was murdered because he knew too much about the CIA's nefarious activities. There were also reports that a professional tennis player, Harold Blauer, had died as a result of being given high doses of mescaline without his consent.

Following these revelations, the United States Army was also investigated and a number of shocking cases came to light in which subjects had been given drugs without their consent or knowledge, as a part of so-called experiments. Legislation was enacted to prevent such abuses occurring again and compensation was paid to some of the victims. Nevertheless, the MKULTRA project remains one of the most sinister, and bizarre, state conspiracies ever to have taken place in America, or perhaps anywhere else.

A CIA document supporting the use of LSD in the MKUltra project.

THE TUSKEGEE

The Tuskegee Syphilis Experiment, which was run between 1932 and 1972, was one of the most shocking scientific studies ever to take place. In it, 399 black men, most of whom were poor Alabaman sharecroppers, took part in a supposed treatment for 'bad blood' which would cure them of illness. They were never told that their illness was syphilis and that – except at the beginning of the study – they were receiving no treatment at all. What was in fact happening was that doctors were studying the ravages of the untreated disease and waiting for them to die so that they could perform autopsies on the corpses. The supposed aim of the experiment was to find out more about the disease and to determine whether it affected black people differently to white people. However, at the end of the study, which continued over several decades, it was suggested that no important knowledge had been yielded. Meanwhile, many men had met their deaths, after terrible illnesses whose symptoms included paralysis, blindness, heart disease, tumours and insanity. Not only this, many of the men's wives had become infected and their children born with congenital syphilis.

'SPECIAL FREE TREATMENT'

The study was started at the Tuskegee Institute, under the auspices of the United States Public Health Service. Its initial aim was to study a group of black men with untreated syphilis for a period of months and then treat the disease. However, several of the doctors wanted to continue the programme for a longer period and fearing that the men would not want to co-operate if they knew the truth – that they were being studied to see how long it took them to die of the disease – the doctors began to misrepresent what was going on. They began to write to their 'patients' advertising 'special free treatment',

Black American combat airmen, 1942, trained under the Tuskegee Air Program. The Tuskegee Syphilis Experiment was less well-publicized, however.

SYPHILIS EXPERIMENT

when all they were doing was performing diagnostic tests. These included painful and dangerous lumbar punctures, from which the patients derived absolutely no medical benefits at all.

SHAMEFUL ETHICS

Penicillin became the standard treatment for syphilis in 1947 and there were government initiatives to treat the population in as rapid a manner as possible. Nationwide campaigns invited citizens to attend treatment centres

and men who were called up into the army were screened for the disease and given treatment. The subjects of the Tuskegee Syphilis Experiment, however, were excluded from the programme but they accepted the story that they were being treated already. In this way, syphilitic men were prevented from gaining treatment that would have saved their lives.

It was not until 1966 that the story broke in the national press. Peter Buxtun, who worked for the Public Health Service in San Francisco as a venereal disease

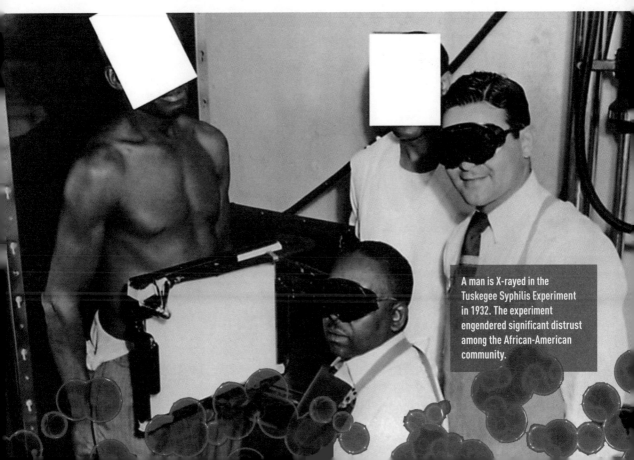

A man is X-rayed in the Tuskegee Syphilis Experiment in 1932. The experiment engendered significant distrust among the African-American community.

investigator, became aware of the experiment and wrote to his superiors to inform them of what was going on. However, he was told that the experiment needed to go ahead and that it would not be curtailed until all the subjects had died and the autopsies had been performed. Frustrated by this brush-off, Buxtun went to the press and in 1972 several national newspapers ran stories on the experiment. The experiment was quickly brought to a halt as a result of the adverse publicity and the surviving subjects and their families compensated and promised free medical treatment in the future.

Two years later, legislation was put into effect to regulate medical experiments involving human beings. However, it was not until 1997 that a public apology was made by the president of the United States. In the presence of the five remaining survivors of the study (only eight were left in total) President Clinton formally apologized for the behaviour of the United States government and called it 'shameful'.

A CONSPIRACY AGAINST ETHNIC MINORITIES

The fact that the study was conducted on black people led many to accuse the scientists who mounted it of racism. However, this was complicated by the fact that several of the staff in charge of the experiment were African-Americans. The experiment was also conducted under the auspices of one of America's most respected black universities, the Tuskegee Institute, set up by Booker T. Washington. The hospital of the university loaned medical facilities to the Public Health Service in order that they could conduct the experiment and local African-American doctors also became involved.

One of the central figures in the drama was a black nurse called Eunice Rivers. She had worked with the subjects for nearly 40 years and was trusted by most of them. Defending her behaviour, she claimed that she was simply carrying out the orders of the doctors and was not in a position to diagnose the patients' illnesses.

A doctor injects a subject with a placebo during the Tuskegee Syphilis Experiment.

Strangely, both black doctors and nurses felt that they were helping solve the problem of venereal disease in the Afro-American community, and they were deeply committed to health programmes that helped the poorest people in their area, Macon County. It was as if they simply could not see that human beings should not be treated in this way, as just a means to an end, even in the cause of supposedly extending medical knowledge.

Also perplexing is the way in which the study was set up. Once it had been dismantled, many questions were asked. Why, for example, had it been thought necessary to find out the differences between the progress of the disease on white people and black people? The study was set up to find out whether it was true that black people experienced cardiovascular problems as a result of syphilis infection, whereas white people were more susceptible to neurological malfunctioning. But how this information would have helped treat the disease remains unclear.

Not only that, but the scientific methodology in the study was flawed. The investigation was designed to show how the disease progressed when untreated but the subjects had already been treated – with contemporary treatments such as mercurial ointments – in the first few months of the programme, before it was decided to extend the study. The thinking behind the experiment was so unclear and the scientific gains were so questionable that one can only assume that an extraordinary level of, possibly unconscious, racism must have blinded the scientists to the fact that they were treating their subjects in a completely inhuman way.

In several later sociological studies the Tuskegee Syphilis Experiment was shown to have had an adverse effect on health programmes directed at African-Americans, who unsurprisingly increasingly mistrusted the public health authorities. The episode caused lasting damage and it is remembered as one of the most appalling conspiracies ever to take place in American history.

Ninety-four-year-old Herman Shaw (R) speaks as US President Bill Clinton looks on during ceremonies at the White House in May 1997, in which Clinton apologized to the survivors and families of the victims of the Tuskegee Syphilis Experiment.

THE CIA AND AIDS

Was HIV, the scourge of world health for two decades, secretly invented by the CIA, the scourge of free people since the 1950s? That's what a surprisingly virulent conspiracy theory holds, one that began almost as soon as the Centers for Disease Control (CDC) unveiled the cause of the mysterious 'gay cancer' cutting a swathe through large urban centres. But unlike many of the more outlandish conspiracy theories of the 1980s and 90s, the idea that the US government had a hand in the creation of the AIDS virus is not based

A poster issued by the US Center for Disease Control in 1993 to warn about the dangers of AIDS.

If Your Man Is Dabbling In Drugs... He Could Be Dabbling With Your Life.

Shooting up or skin popping, if your man is sharing needles he could get the AIDS virus and bring it home to you. So if he's running with the drug crowd, even if it's only on the weekends, you need to talk to him. Try to get him into counselling. Insist that he wear a condom every time you have sex. And if he's not listening to you —do something to save your life. Leave.

For more information about AIDS, call:
NATIONAL AIDS HOTLINE
1-800-342-AIDS
Servicio en Espanol
1-800-344-7432
TTY-Deaf Access
1-800-243-7889

AMERICA RESPONDS TO AIDS

 U.S. DEPARTMENT OF HEALTH AND HUMAN SERVICES
Public Health Service   CDC

merely on unsourced accounts and incomprehensible arguments. There were serious concerns early in the AIDS epidemic that the government was dragging its feet on research and treatment, and that the disease was most prevalent among the populations that white evangelical America had the most trouble with: homosexuals, drug users and African Americans.

And unlike many other conspiracy theories of the time, this one garnered attention far beyond the US and Western Europe. The conspiracy still has a massive impact on AIDS treatment and prevention in the developing world, sowing distrust in new medications and government-run prevention campaigns. In South Africa, the United States' involvement in AIDS is such a given that nearly a third of gay men in Cape Town believe it. And in the US, a 2005 survey found that nearly 50 per cent of black men think HIV was man-made, and that a cure for the disease was being withheld from the poor so they could be used as medical guinea pigs.

Where do these theories come from? Why would so many people believe that the US government created and unleashed a weapon to cull certain parts of the population, while simultaneously researching new treatments for it?

A TERRIFYING NEW DISEASE REQUIRES NEW EXPLANATIONS

The conspiracy theory that the US created AIDS as a weapon has its origins in something that should be familiar to any follower of contemporary politics:

Russian disinformation. And it started in 1983, before the origin of AIDS as caused by HIV had been scientifically confirmed. Seeking to play on the fears of both minority communities in the US and people in the developing world, the KGB began an organized campaign to make people think that the US had invented AIDS to cull those deemed to be undesirables.

It began with an anonymous letter in a pro-Soviet newspaper in India supposedly from an American scientist claiming that AIDS had been bio-engineered in the US Army's chemical weapons lab at Fort Detrick, Maryland in 1977 and 1978. More Soviet puppet media figures pushed the story out into African news outlets, and by 1987 it was being covered on the CBS Evening News. By that point, the American conspiracy theory community latched on to it, with alternative medicine practitioner William Campbell Douglass claiming that the World Health Organization invented AIDS to cleanse Africa for colonization in his 1989 book *AIDS: The End of Civilization*. William Cooper's famous 1991 conspiracy tome *Behold a Pale Horse* used misconstrued Congressional testimony to 'prove' that the US had been developing 'a new infective micro-organism' since 1969, and blaming it on a coalition of powerful elites and Jews.

The Soviet disinformation campaign was enormously successful. By the mid-1980s it was practically common knowledge among black populations that AIDS was an American biological agent run amok in populations that were denigrated and marginalized under the Reagan administration.

Building 470 at Fort Detrick was the location of America's biological weapons research programme.

And the theory had celebrity adherents. Bill Cosby claimed in 1992 that if AIDS 'wasn't created to get rid of black folks, it sure likes us a lot', while Will Smith speculated that AIDS was 'possibly created as a result of biological-warfare testing'. Nation of Islam leader Louis Farrakhan claimed that new AIDS therapies like AZT were part of the conspiracy as well. African news and politics were full of accusations that the US and/or white South African doctors were smearing condoms with HIV, using it to poison food and pollute rivers, and even testing new forms of the disease disguised as cures – causing a deep vein of suspicion against white doctors, their diseases and their drugs.

REASON TO BE SUSPICIOUS

While these seem like implausible plots full of assumed details, there are good reasons to be suspicious of the American government's role in medical research. In 1932, the Public Health Service began a six-month experiment on African American men in rural Alabama to study syphilis. But it misled its subjects into giving informed consent, and faked their treatments, lasting decades after a cure for syphilis was widely available (see pages 186–9). The lies went on for 40 years. At the same time, the CIA was experimenting with hallucinogenic drugs and mind control as part of the MKULTRA project (see pages 182–5), often on unwitting subjects.

Thanks to a harsh media spotlight and outrage from Congress, both of these illegal human experiments became public knowledge in the mid-1970s, only a few years before the first Soviet conspiracies about AIDS.

It's not surprising that the African American community embraced these conspiracy theories. AIDS was first confirmed in 1981, but it took until 1985 for Ronald Reagan to acknowledge its existence, in a press conference where he hinted that children born with HIV shouldn't be allowed to stay in school with non-infected children. At the height of the conspiracy, the mid to late 1990s, the government had long shifted its stance on AIDS, and treatments for HIV were available – but were expensive and hard to get. And AIDS still was far more prevalent in marginalized communities than in the white middle class mainstream. Even after a decade, African Americans represented nearly 50 per cent of new HIV cases diagnosed in the United States, far outstripping their demographic percentage.

AN IMPOSSIBLE TIMELINE

The conspiracy theory is falsified by the very nature of how AIDS works. The trajectory of a disease that takes between 10 and 15 years to manifest simply doesn't match up with the conspiracy theory that the US created it in 1977. By 1981, when the CDC identified that AIDS had become an epidemic, it had been in

William Campbell Douglass claimed that the World Health Organization was responsible for creating AIDS.

the early 1960s in Africa, and it entered New York in the early 1970s, mistaken for virulent pneumonia. The epidemic was in full bloom when the conspiracy says it began. Beyond that, if AIDS was meant to purge gay men and drug users, it failed. There are now treatments for HIV that render it a chronic illness, rather than a fatal disease – though it still requires a daily regimen of multiple expensive medications to control.

And if the CIA did indeed invent AIDS, it didn't bother protecting its own agents very well. According to declassified documents, it wasn't until 1987 that the agency began alerting personnel in high-risk countries about the potential for contracting HIV from sexual encounters, and it didn't start testing prospective employees until later that year. By that point, the AIDS epidemic was already in full swing, likely claiming the lives of CIA agents as well as the population it was supposedly created to wipe out. Ultimately, the CIA creating AIDS is a plausible conspiracy theory not because of its mechanics, but because of the people involved – and that's not, in and of itself, proof of a conspiracy.

the US population for a decade. We now have a fairly well established chain of events for how it originated, starting with cross-species transmission of the simian immunodeficiency virus from primates to humans, possibly as early as the 1920s. The first deaths from what later became identified as AIDS took place in

Ronald Reagan is handed a report of the presidential commission on AIDS by James D. Watkins. Reagan did not acknowledge the existence of the disease until 1985, four years after it had been identified as an epidemic.

FLAT EARTH

After persisting as a fringe movement for decades, the belief that Earth is actually flat, and not a globe, and that the entire scientific establishment is lying to all of us, suddenly experienced a massive spike in popularity in early 2015.

What drove this surge isn't clear. It's certainly not anything that could be construed as a new scientific discovery – since the scientific community has known for 2,500 years that the world is round. It's far more likely that it's a combination of social media, general distrust in institutions and the decline of critical thinking in Western society that's caused a not-small number of people to think the Earth is flat.

And yet, they do. The new 'flat Earth' movement has drawn tens of thousands of people into various Facebook groups, spawned countless popular YouTube videos and debates, caught the eye of minor celebrities and even forced popular science communicators to respond to it.

Surveys back up this disturbing trend. A February 2018 survey from YouGov asked 8,200 Americans if they 'believe that the world is round or flat', and only 84 per cent answered that they had never believed the Earth wasn't round. It also showed that 2 per cent of Americans believe with no doubt that the Earth is flat, and as many as one-third of those aged 18 to 24 either harbour some doubt that the Earth is round, or weren't sure either way.

The evidence for it depends on scientific concepts that are either wilfully misunderstood or simply made up. When cornered, many flat Earthers fall back on insults, generic arguments to 'do your own research', or change the subject.

But is there any evidence? Or is the flat Earth movement merely one designed to decentralize knowledge and put very basic scientific concepts (such as what the Earth looks like) into the hands of the people who recently had knowledge handed down to them from on high?

WHAT DOES A FLAT EARTH LOOK LIKE?

Contrary to popular misconception, neither ancient people nor those living afterwards believed the Earth

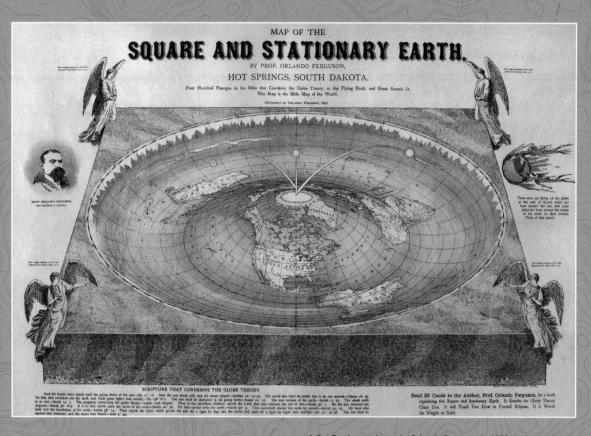

A flat Earth map drawn by Orlando Ferguson in 1893. It shows the Antarctic as a wall of ice surrounding the edge of the world.

was flat. While many ancient societies did depict the planet as flat and surrounded by water, by the 5th century BC, the Greeks had carried out rudimentary experiments proving that the Earth was a globe, though they didn't know how big it was.

The great Pythagoras was involved in some of the earliest efforts to prove the Earth was round. Likewise, Aristotle noted that various signs of a spherical Earth, such as how ships disappear over the horizon and the position of stars moving, 'show not only that the Earth is circular in shape, but also that it is a sphere of no great size: for otherwise the effect of so slight a change of place would not be so quickly apparent.'

Nor did Christopher Columbus go 'sailing the ocean blue' to prove that the Earth was round. That bit of lore came from a story by Washington Irving. And Galileo wasn't sent to his death for disputing the Catholic Church's belief in a flat Earth, as Thomas Jefferson wrongly wrote a century earlier.

Flat Earth mythos was mostly the stuff of arguments between various religious factions until the late 1800s,

when a book called *Zetetic Astronomy: The Earth not a Globe* articulated the claim that the planet was a flat disc surrounded by ice walls – with hell itself lying beyond those icy cliffs. That book, written by Samuel Rowbotham under the pseudonym 'Parallax', took off in certain English circles and spawned a debating society and several well-known attempts by believers to prove the flatness of the Earth. Eventually, the Zetetic movement became more about opposition to established science in general, and it died out after World War I.

But its basic tenets were picked up by an English sign painter in the 1950s, who founded the International Flat Earth Research Society based on the Zetetic movement – though not sharing much of its actual beliefs. That group eventually turned into a purely non-scientific Christian fundamentalist conspiracy mongering group, and then into an online only forum dedicated to conspiracy theories, which now has about 11,000 members and doesn't talk much about flat Earth.

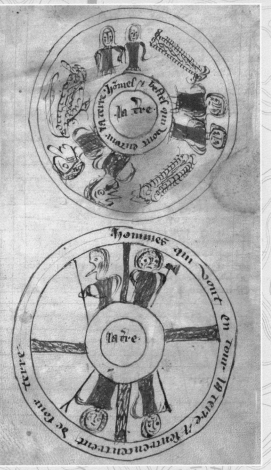

Contrary to popular belief, in the Middle Ages most people believed the Earth to be round. This image from a fourteenth-century manuscript depicts a spherical Earth.

ZETETIC ASTRONOMY.

EARTH NOT A GLOBE!

AN EXPERIMENTAL INQUIRY

INTO THE

TRUE FIGURE OF THE EARTH:

PROVING IT A PLANE,

WITHOUT AXIAL OR ORBITAL MOTION;

AND THE

ONLY MATERIAL WORLD

IN

THE UNIVERSE!

BY "PARALLAX."

London:
SIMPKIN, MARSHALL, AND CO., STATIONERS' HALL COURT.
Bath:
S HAYWARD, GREEN STREET.
1865.

[The Right of Translation is Reserved by the Author.]

The front cover of *Zetetic Astronomy*, written by the flat Earth campaigner Samuel Rowbotham, who went by the pseudonym Parallax.

WHAT DO FLAT EARTHERS BELIEVE?

The basics of flat Earth belief vary, but generally, you're likely to find most believers think the Earth is some kind of flat disc, and that the scientific establishment has lied to us about what our senses 'really' tell us.

Many flat Earth debates become entangled in minute aspects of science and weather that most people don't understand. The depth and detail of these discussions ends up lending credence to what they discuss, as if any scientific theory that wasn't true simply couldn't have as much sheer material to debate. Part of this debate revolves around the misuse of scientific jargon, deploying concepts like 'crepuscular rays' (sunbeams shining through clouds) proving that the sun must be much closer to the Earth, and gyroscopic attitude indicators on planes staying horizontal during flights.

These are real things, but are totally misinterpreted by flat Earth believers.

To explain away the vast amount of pictures of Earth as a globe, they just claim every photo of a 'globular' Earth was either distorted by a fisheye lens, or faked. They also throw out things that are true, but have perfectly reasonable explanations, such as there being no direct flights across the South Pole from Chile to New Zealand, that large bodies of water don't wobble due to spinning, or that it's impossible to see the curve of the Earth at the height commercial airlines are allowed to fly at. Indeed, long lists of such 'proofs' of flat Earth are the lingua franca of the movement, demanding enormous time and effort to debunk – hence few people doing it.

Beyond that, the bigger a flat disc is, the more distorted the gravity becomes away from its centre,

The flat earth conference in Denver, November 2018. The flat Earth movement has grown rapidly in popularity since 2015.

which is why galaxies are flat with spiral arms. On a flat Earth, weather and daytime would function totally differently, because of distorted gravity. Many flat Earthers claim that gravity itself is also a hoax, and the flat Earth is accelerating upwards, propelled by 'universal acceleration'. This is not a concept that has ever been proven to be possible. But it's central to flat Earth, and is the only thing that would explain why the sun rises and sets over a flat Earth, or why the stars change their positions.

Some flat Earthers seem to understand how little evidence there is in favour of their argument, and are less interested in trying to thrash out the intricacies of things like why the Earth would be the only flat planet in the solar system, and are more interested in simply questioning everything around them. Indeed, flat Earth beliefs are almost entirely intertwined with conspiracy theory beliefs as a whole, which is consistent with established research showing that if you believe one conspiracy theory, you're likely to believe others. Believers spend as much of their online time talking about 'waking up' and 'doing research' in general as they do about flat Earth in particular. They distrust scientific authorities, governments and popular figures who tell us to assume the Earth is round. They put their faith in their senses, their biases and what they want to be true, rather than what others tell them. And there's a nasty strain of anti-Semitism in the flat Earth movement, like there is in almost every moderately popular conspiracy theory.

In the end, any time spent in the flat Earth community reveals that it's hard to tell who truly believes it, who's just there for laughs and who will believe any conspiracy theory put in front of them as long as it implicates 'the powers that be'.

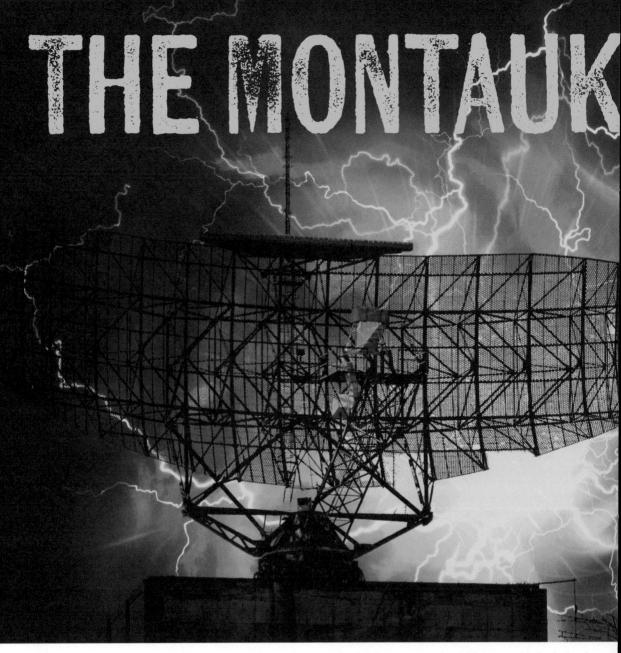

THE MONTAUK

On a remote tip of Long Island, New York, in the hamlet of Montauk, stands either a relic of World War II fears, or an ultra-sophisticated scientific base devoted to some of the most terrifying research in American history. The place is ostensibly called Camp Hero, and is now a state park. But according to an almost limitless series of books, TV documentaries and websites, the US government used Camp Hero to research time travel, the opening of other-worldly portals, the enhancement of latent psychic abilities and psychological warfare. All of this went on for decades,

until a few courageous whistleblowers published a book in the early 1990s blowing the lid off the whole evil thing.

What's called 'the Montauk Project' took off just as the conspiracy theory community was making the leap on to the internet. It encompasses a wide range of supposedly secret technology being harnessed by an evil government for sinister purposes, and equally little evidence to support their existence. And these secrets, paradoxically, are reported on so extensively that they are almost common knowledge now. But the

PROJECT

Montauk Project is also so compelling to mainstream audiences that it's spawned the hit TV series *Stranger Things*, multiple reality TV shows and countless books. There must be something to the strange doings at Camp Hero that fires the public imagination, even if the more outlandish claims are shrouded in mystery.

Or maybe that's just what they want us to think.

THE HORRORS OF CAMP HERO

Montauk, New York, has a population of just 3,300 people. But its location makes it one of the most strategically important places on the East Coast. The early American military built the Montauk Lighthouse to keep watch for British ships trying to enter Long Island Sound, while during World War II, the navy turned Montauk into a 112-hectare base full of coastal artillery, docks and planes. That base was named Camp Hero, after a recently deceased Army Chief of Coast Artillery, and would serve as one of the first points of

The decommissioned radar station at Camp Hero in Montauk, New York.

contact should the Axis try to invade New York. The invasion never came, and in keeping with changing technology, Camp Hero was converted into a state-of-the-art radar installation meant to pick up incoming Soviet bombers and missiles. But by 1984, even that threat had largely passed, and Camp Hero was shut down and donated to the state for future use as a park and ecological reserve.

The closure of a fairly sophisticated military facility sparked conspiracy theories that were eventually collected in the 1992 book *The Montauk Project: Experiments in Time*, written by Preston Nichols and Peter Moon. The authors allege, based on Nichols' repressed memories being recovered, that Camp Hero was home to a top-secret experiment. Called the Phoenix Project, it continued work that the US government first began in the 1940s with the 'Philadelphia Experiment', a plot to make a naval warship invisible, only to have it drive its crew to mental breakdown. Funded by Nazi gold, the Phoenix Project built a massive bunker under the camp, and used it to test mind control technology by subjecting kidnapped orphans to massive hits of electromagnetic radiation from a thought-transforming device they called the 'Montauk Chair'. At the same time, the government used secret technology developed by Nikola Tesla to break down the barriers between time and space, once even making a quantum interlock with the original Philadelphia Experiment and bringing two sailors forward in time over 40 years. There were also rumours of alien ships, teleportation, involvement by the Nazi 'Order of the Black Sun', the building of a '50-foot titanium ziggurat' on the grounds, and young boys reprogrammed into super soldiers to be unleashed at the right time. Finally, when the time portal created at Montauk began disgorging terrifying creatures from other dimensions, Nichols could stand no more. He smashed the 'Montauk Chair' and many of the most arcane and horrible experiments ended. No more kidnapped orphans, no more time portals.

Or did they end? In 2008, the carcass of a bizarre creature washed on to the shore of Montauk, a beast

quickly dubbed the 'Montauk Monster' by the media, and deemed proof that whatever the Montauk Chair brought through the portal was real – and maybe still around.

STRANGER THINGS – BUT NOT THAT STRANGE

Despite its scattershot approach and lack of evidence, the Montauk Project conspiracy theory took off. After all, the government was already involved in terrible experiments involving mind control and drugs, under the MKULTRA umbrella. And the Cold War was a desperate time where the threat of nuclear annihilation pushed the US to develop weapons once seen only in science fiction. So why couldn't this be true, too? Buoyed by its initial success in the conspiracy community, Nichols and Moon churned out an endless series of Montauk books and allegations, including a sequel

two years later, and other books about the 'pyramids of Montauk', the Nazi connection to Montauk and links to aliens from the Pleiades Cluster. Other writers soon took their work and spun it into even more bizarre directions.

As the years went on, the Montauk Project got bigger, more expansive and less plausible. Its 'time tunnel' was said to have changed the outcome of the Civil War, it was supposedly the birthplace of the Men in Black, the headquarters of the 'black helicopters' used by the government against citizens, and where the legendary Jersey Devil monster was spawned. Others accused it of being where the moon landing hoax was filmed, and even where AIDS was invented. Nikola Tesla was alleged to be running the experiments there, despite having been dead for decades, using a staff entirely of Nazi scientists. The conspiracy theories became so expansive that there was simply no credible way for one

205409

The Jersey Devil is one of many strange occurrences that has since been attributed to the Montauk project.

place to have spawned all of its evil deeds, particularly a place as small and isolated as Camp Hero. It strains even the logic of conspiracy theories that one place could be the site of a 'time tunnel', mind control experiments, psychic chambers and biological laboratories. One, maybe. But all of them?

The authors of the original Montauk Project book never let go of their claims, with Nichols asserting the Montauk story until his death in 2018. And finding a rich vein of fringe material, Hollywood came calling, giving even more credibility to Nichols and Moon. Elements of *Men in Black* and *The X-Files* were based on Montauk mythology, and *Stranger Things* not only used huge parts of the psychic child soldier/dimensional portal mythos, but was even called 'Montauk' early in its development. But none of it has ever been proven to be real. Camp Hero is now a park and wildlife refuge that gets hundreds of thousands of visitors – and not

one has found any evidence of anything the Montauk Project authors allege. Likewise, the Philadelphia Experiment that supposedly formed the basis for the Montauk Project has never been proven to have taken place, while the Montauk Monster of 2008 was almost certainly a decayed raccoon.

Montauk speaks to our desire to see the dark hand of government control in every strange happening, even if they didn't actually happen. But it's also a window into our need for great stories full of bizarre events, heroic whistleblowers, larger than life danger and evil villains in lab coats who come for our children. Montauk has them all. The Montauk Project might remain a myth, but it's powered by some of the oldest notions in the human psyche. And that's why it retains its power.

CERN

Located deep underneath the border between France and Switzerland lies a massive metal ring, full of pipes, wires, sensors and other sophisticated equipment. The nearly 27 km (17 mile) loop, known as the Large Hadron Collider (LHC), is the most complex scientific instrument ever built, and was designed to replicate the conditions that existed in the universe in the moments after the Big Bang. But some believe its true purpose to be much darker – a way for scientists to touch the most evil forces known, and unleash pure terror on the people. Artificial earthquakes, portals to hell itself, directed energy weapons, mind control, alternate dimensions, microscopic black holes, even human sacrifice to ancient gods: all are suspected as the true purpose of the LHC, and its parent organization, CERN.

The CERN research centre in Switzerland, where the Large Hadron Collider is located. To some it represents the pinnacle of scientific research. To others, it is the home of a sinister conspiracy.

The size, scope and cost of the LHC all make it rife for conspiracy theories. It's a hugely expensive piece of scientific equipment that does things in the middle of nowhere that most people don't understand – giving us a clearer picture of the origin of the universe, as well as gigantic amounts of data to study. Through it all, though, misinformation and conspiracy theories persist, with fringe books and mainstream websites alike pushing out stories that are either misunderstandings of the work done there, or are simply false.

So what does CERN really do at the LHC? Is it a doorway to evil? Or a window into the birth of our reality?

'TOTAL EXISTENCE FAILURE'

It's important to distinguish between CERN, the French acronym for the European Organization for Nuclear Research, and the Large Hadron Collider. Formed in 1954, CERN has 22 member states, has been awarded the Nobel Prize in Physics, and was the site of some of the earliest research for the world wide web. It's also where the Higgs boson, known as the 'God particle', was confirmed after decades of research. But the LHC captured the imaginations of both the general public and the conspiracy theory community because of both its incredible cost and its purpose. It's designed to crash combined subatomic particles (known as 'hadrons') together at such speeds that they'll create new high-energy particles only known to exist at the dawn of time – shedding light on fundamental questions in physics and cosmology. As such, the LHC attracted conspiracy theories well before it was even activated. Fringe Christian theorists claimed that the LHC was actually opening a portal to hell, based on interpretations of biblical texts and strange-looking clouds over the LHC site. The theory proved so popular that YouTube videos espousing it have racked up millions of views.

There were also fears that such meddling with the primal forces of nature might have devastating effects, including earthquakes, plasma storms and even destroying every molecule in the universe, a kind of 'total existence failure' only seen in apocalyptic science fiction. After all, nobody had previously attempted to recreate the energy of the dawn of the universe, so nobody could prove what would or wouldn't happen. The fact that the LHC was beset with delays, malfunctions and cost overruns even led some people to believe that there were higher powers trying to prevent the machine from being turned on. The most famous was a 2009 incident where a bird flew into the underground chamber and dropped

The Large Hadron Collider at CERN has been blamed for everything from creating black holes to acting as an altar for human sacrifice to ancient gods.

a bit of bread into the electrical power system that ran the device's super-cooled magnets. Two esteemed scientists published a paper accusing the bird and other maladies of 'reverse chronological causation' – or that the LHC sent waves back in time causing it to try to turn itself off.

Despite the efforts of the time-travelling bird, the LHC was indeed activated, firing its first particle collisions a few months later. And the conspiracy theories have continued ever since. One popular theory is that the LHC has shifted humanity into an alternate dimension, and that the phenomenon of the 'Mandela Effect', where large masses remember events that never actually took place, is fragments of our original dimension reasserting themselves. There are also the usual accusations of CERN conducting time travel experiments, creating portals for alien spacecraft, trying to open 'quantum black holes' and summoning ancient demons foretold in the Revelation of John. Finally, there was the human sacrifice video that made the rounds in 2016, supposedly showing a candle lit ceremony at the base of a statue of Shiva located on the grounds of CERN that ended with a ritual murder. While not all of these conspiracy theories could be true, couldn't at least a few? After all, how do you fake earthquakes and murder?

ALIENS AND WEASELS

Most of the theories about CERN and the LHC are based on a fundamental misunderstanding of physics, which is excusable, since particle physics is beyond most people's comprehension. It takes decades of training to understand concepts like the Higgs boson, pentaquarks and the strong and weak nuclear forces. But anyone can grab on to conspiracy theories like the destruction of the universe or a tunnel to hell. They require no training at all, just an imagination and preconceived biases. Because of the widespread appeal of CERN conspiracy theories, they're a pop culture stalwart. CERN and the LHC have been depicted on TV on *The Big Bang Theory*, *Ancient Aliens* and *Doctor Who*, along with the massively popular book *The Da Vinci Code*. They

The statue of Shiva outside CERN was supposedly the site of ritual sacrifice, recorded in a video in 2016. The video was later revealed to be a hoax.

show CERN as unleashing horrific events like suicide epidemics, alien invasions and even mass zombification. Yet, paradoxically, there are viral videos made by CERN employees depicting exactly what the LHC does, and how amazing it is. CERN has also granted open access to its research to thousands of libraries, universities and scientific institutions.

While the 'human sacrifice' video turned out to be a prank, some of these conspiracy theories do at least have a grain of truth to them. The LHC was beset by problems and overspending, with its original opening, planned for November 2007, delayed for two years – culminating in the bread-bombing bird incident. The accidents didn't stop even after activation, as a weasel got into the electrical circuitry and caused a short that shut the LHC down briefly. But while there was no molecular collapse of the universe, there were mysterious earthquakes all over the world, from Italy and Switzerland to New Zealand, which CERN was forced to deny responsibility for; along with a mysterious seismic event in November 2018 where earthquake monitors detected 20 minutes of shaking with no apparent cause.

Pinning the blame for every one of these incidents, real and imagined alike, on CERN is just lazy conspiracy navel-gazing. No matter how fast subatomic particles are crashed together, they can't make earthquakes, control minds or open time portals. And even if they could, there would have been a pause in them, because in November 2018, CERN announced the LHC would be shutting down for two years to perform upgrades and process the vast amount of data it had already collected. While it's possible that CERN simply wanted to use the break to make more efficient hell portals and earthquake devices, it's more likely that they wanted to make sure that the LHC, already the coolest scientific instrument around, was even cooler for experiments to come. Trying to shed light on the beginning of the universe deserves nothing less than the most sophisticated machines available to humanity. And while they were at it, maybe they could do something to keep animals out.

An engineer works on the Large Hadron Collider. Seismic tremors across the world in 2016 forced CERN to issue a statement denying responsibility for them.

INDEX

Abeltsev, Sergei 28
Agenda 21 134–7
Agenda 21 (Beck) 137
AIDS 190–3
AIDS: The End of Civilization (Douglas) 191
Al-Fayed, Dodi 55, 56
Al-Fayed, Mohammed 55, 56–7
al-Qaeda 27
Alioto, Joe 92
Allen, Gary 105
Allende, Salvador 120–3
Ameer, Leon 4X 53
Andrade, Noberto 28
Angels Don't Play This HAARP: Advances in Tesla Technology (Begich) 32, 33
Area 51 162–5
Armstrong, Neil 158
Arnold, Kenneth 141
Beck, Glenn 136, 137
Begich, Nick 32–3
Behold a Pale Horse (Cooper) 191
Bell, Art 33
Bender, Albert K. 156
Berezovsky, Boris 26, 27
Berlin Christmas market attack 131
Bernstein, Carl 112
Bernstein, Herman 88
Bezos, Jeff 69
Biarritz (Goedsche) 86
Biggest Secret, The (Icke) 95–6
Bilderberg Group 10, 68–71
Bin Laden, Osama 70
Blauer, Harold 185
Blowing Up Russia (Litvinenko) 27
Body Snatchers in the Desert (Redfern) 145
Bond, Bryce 152
Bower, Doug 152
Brazel, William 'Mack' 141
Brevik, Anders 131
Brown, Dan 10, 85
Brown, Ron 64
Brussell, Mae 90
Bulge, Battle of the 129
Bush, George H. W. 105

Bush, George W. 64, 65
Butler, Norman 3X 52
Buxtun, Peter 187–8
Cabot, Henry 134
Caesar, Julius 8
Calo, Pippo 79, 80
Calvi, Roberto 10, 78–81
Cameron, Ewan 185
Capone, Al 48
Carboni, Flavio 79, 80
Caruana, Stephanie 90, 92
Castro, Fidel 48, 70, 121
Cedra, Aguirre 121
Central Intelligence Agency (CIA) 15, 16, 48, 59–60, 61, 92, 120–3, 127, 162, 164, 179–80, 182–5, 190–3
CERN research centre 202–5
Chapman, Mark 59–61
Chappaquiddick 9, 124–7
Charles, Prince 55, 69
Charlie Hebdo shootings 131
chemtrails 38–41
Chorley, Dave 152
Clapper, James 17
Clinton, Bill 62–5, 69, 189
Clinton Body Count 62–5
Clinton, Hillary 62–5, 69
Connally, John B. 45, 46
Cooper, William 191
Copeland, David 70
Corrocher, Teresa 80
Cosby, Bill 192
Crimmins, John 125
crop circles 150–3
Cruz, Ted 137
Da Vinci Code, The (Brown) 10, 85
da Vinci, Leonardo 85
Dahl, Harold 156
Dannemeyer, William 63–4
Dean, John 113, 115
Di Carlo, Francesco 79–80
Diana, Princess of Wales 6, 54–7
'Dialogues in Hell Between Machiavelli and Montesquieu' (Joly) 86
Dice, Mark 105
Diotallevi, Ernesto 79, 80
Douglass, William Campbell 191
Dubose, Thomas 144

Dulles, Alan 48, 183
Dunning, Brian 99
ELF waves 30–3
Enron 6
Exon, Arthur 142, 144
false flags 128–33
Farrakhan, Louis 53, 89, 192
Farrar, John 126
Federal Bureau of Investigation (FBI) 24, 33, 48, 59–61, 92, 174, 176–7, 179–80
Federal Security Service (FSB) 26, 27
flat Earth theory 194–7
Flight MH370 9, 18–21
Ford, Henry 88
Foster, Vince 62, 64
Freemasons 8, 75, 76, 79, 80
Friedman, Stanton 142
Gargan, Joe 125, 126
Gates, Bill 69, 70
Gelli, Licio 79, 80
Gemstone Files 90–3
Ghorbanifar, Manucher 118
Goedsche, Hermann 86, 88
Golovinski, Matvei 86
Gorbachev, Mikhail 105
Gottleib, Sidney 183, 184
Government Communications Headquarters (GCHQ) 15, 17, 23, 24
Guardian, The 17
Gulf of Tonkin incident 130
HAARP 30–3
Hague, William 24
Halliburton 6
Hayer, Talmadge 52, 53
Heflin, Rex 157
Helpern, Milton 52
Hitler, Adolf 6, 88–9, 99, 130
Holy Blood, Holy Grail (Baigent *et al.*) 84
Holy Grail 6, 10–11, 83–4
Hoover, J. Edgar 48, 59
Hopkins, Herbert 156
Hughes, Howard 92, 93
Icke, David 95–7
Illuminati 6, 49, 72–7
In God's Name (Yallop) 81
Iran-Contra affair 116–19

John Paul I, Pope 80–1
Johnson, Lyndon B. 47, 48, 92, 130
Johnson, Thomas 15X 52
Joly, Maurice 86, 88
Jones, Alex 69, 70, 75
Joseph of Arimathea 83, 84
Joyal, Paul 28
Junot, Philippe 56
Karpichkov, Boris 24, 25
Kavanaugh, Brett 64
Keith, Bill 92
Kennedy, Jacqueline 48–9
Kennedy, Edward 92, 124–7
Kennedy, John F. 6, 9, 44–9, 92, 127
Kennedy, Robert 124, 127
Keough, Rosemary 124–5
King, Martin Luther 50
Kissinger, Henry 69, 70, 121, 122, 123
Kleinzig, Manuela 79, 80
Knights Templar 83, 84, 85
Kopechne, Mary Jo 124–7
Koresh, David 172, 173, 174, 176
Kovtun, Dmitry 27–8
La Rosa, Raymond 125
Large Hadron Collidor (LHC) 202–5
Las Vegas Strip attack 131, 132
Lazar, Bob 165
League of Nations 134
Lenin, Vladimir 86
Lennon, John 6, 58–61
Liddy, Gordon 113
Lieder, Nancy 167–8
Litvinenko, Alexander 6, 26–8
Look, Christopher 125, 126
Lowell, Percival 167
Lugovoy, Andrei 27–8
Lyons, Maryellen 124
Lyons, Nance 124
Macron, Emanuel 69
Mafia 10, 47–8, 90, 92
Magdalene Conspiracy 84–5
Magdalene, Mary 84
Mailliez, Doctor 56–7
Maine, USS 130
Malcolm X 9, 50–3
Marcel, Jesse 141, 142, 143

Marcinkus, Paul 79, 80
Markham, Paul 125, 126
McCord, James W. 111, 112, 113
McFarlane, Robert 118, 119
McNulty, Michael 176
McVeigh, Timothy 70, 106, 177
Meade, David 169
men in black 154–7
Merkel, Angela 15, 69
Mitchell, John 112, 113
MKULTRA programme 182–5, 200
Monroe, Marilyn 6, 9
Montauk Project 198–201
Montauk Project, The: Experiments in Time (Nichols and Moon) 199
Moon landings 158–61
Moon, Peter 199, 200, 201
Moore, William 142
Muhammad, Elijah 53
Mukden Incident 130
Mysteries of the People, The (Sue) 86
National Security Agency (NSA) 15, 16–17
Nazarbayev, Nursultan 19
New World Order 104–7
New World Order, The (Robertson) 105–6
New World Order, The: Facts & Fiction (Dice) 105
Newburgh, Esther 125
Newton, Isaac 85
Ngo Dinh Diem 48
Nibiru/Planet X 166–9
Nichols, Preston 199, 200, 201
Nichols, Terry 106
Nixon, Richard 92, 110–15, 123
North, Oliver 116, 117, 118, 119
Obama, Barack 33, 64, 95, 96–7
Oklahoma City bombing 106, 107, 177
Olsen, Frank 185
Onassis, Aristotle 49, 90, 92–3
Ono, Yoko 59
Oswald, Lee Harvey 6, 45, 46, 47, 48
Paul, Henri 55, 56
Pearl Harbor 6
Philip IV, King 83
Pinochet, Augustus 121–2, 123

Plantard, Pierre 85
Poindexter, John 117, 118, 119
Politkovskaya, Anna 27
Primakov, Yevgeny 193
Priory of Sion 85
Prodi, Romano 27
Protocols of the Elders of Zion 86–9
Pulse Nightclub massacre 131
Putin, Vladimir 19, 26, 27, 29, 131
Q-Ships 129
Randle, Kevin 144
Razak, Najib 19
Reagan, Ronald 59, 117, 118, 119, 192, 193
Redfern, Nick 145
Rees Jones, Trevor 55
Reichstag Fire 6, 7, 130
Rendlesham affair 146–9
Reno, Janet 174
reptile elite 94–7
RFID chips 34–7
Rivers, Eunice 188–9
Roberts, Bruce 90
Roberts, Gene 52
Robertson, Pat 105–6
Rockefeller, David 70
Roden, Benjamin 173
Roden, Lois 173
Rojcewicz, Peter 156–7
Roswell Incident 140–5
Rothschild banking family 98–103
Rothschild, Mayer Amschel 98, 99, 101, 102–3
Rothschild, Nathan 98–9, 102
Rothschild, Salomon 99
Rowbotham, Samuel 195
Ruby, Jack 45, 48
Sandy Hook shootings 131
Saunière, François Bérenger 84–5
Sawers, Sir John 24
Scaramella, Mario 27
Schmitt, Donald 144
Schmitt, Harrison Hagan 160
Schneider, René 123
Sebire, Jackie 24
Secret Intelligence Service (MI6) 23, 24
Shaw, Herman 189

Shuttlewood, Arthur 152
Sindona, Michele 79
Sirica, John 113
Sitchin, Zecharia 167
Skripal, Sergei 29
Skripal, Yulia 29
Sleppy, Lydia 142
Smathers, George 124
Snowden, Edward 14–17
Spychips Threat, The 35
Stephenson, Sir Paul 24
Sue, Eugène 86
Tannenbaum, Susan 124
Tesla, Nikola 32, 199, 200
Theodore, Charles 76, 77
Thompson, Linda 63–4, 65
Trepashkin, Mikhail 26, 27

Tretter, Charles 125
Trump, Donald 33, 64
Truth Shall Set You Free, The (Icke) 97
Tuskegee Syphilis Experiment 186–9
TWA Flight 800 178–81
United Nations 134–7
Ventura, Jesse 31, 32
Viaux, Roberto 123
von Braun, Wernher 161
Waco 106, 172–7
Waco: The Big Lie (film) 63
Warren Commission 44–5, 49
Watergate 9, 110–15
Weinberger, Caspar 118, 119
Weishaupt, Adam 75, 76

White, George Hunter 184
Wilcox, Fiona 24
Wilcox, Sherrif 141
Wilhelm I of Hesse 99, 101
Williams, Gareth 22–5
Williams, Gordon 146
Wills, Frank 110–11
Wilson, Woodrow 104, 105
Wise, Jeff 19, 21
Wolf, Lucien 88
Woodward, Bob 112
Wyden, Ron 17
Yallop, David 81
Zetetic Astronomy (Rowbotham) 195
Ziegler, Ron 112

PICTURE CREDITS

t = top, b = bottom, l = left, r = right, m = middle

Alamy: 41, 124, 126, 187, 191, 201

Bridgeman Images: 196l

Corbis: 28, 116, 127

ESO: 166, 168

Getty Images: 16, 20, 21, 29, 31, 37, 44, 45, 51, 53b, 54, 58, 62, 64, 65, 68, 69, 70, 71 (x2), 81b, 83, 84, 87b, 89, 108, 112, 115, 129, 130, 131, 136, 157, 158, 159, 160, 164b, 165t, 178, 180 (x2), 186, 189, 193b, 197, 205

National Archives and Records Administration, USA: 46b

Press Association: 22, 24, 26

Rex Features: 25, 48, 49t, 52, 56, 57, 60, 61 (x2), 152, 163t, 172, 175, 176, 177

Shutterstock: 9, 11, 12, 14, 17, 18, 23, 32r, 34, 35, 36, 39, 40, 42, 46t, 47, 55, 59, 63, 66, 72, 73, 74, 80, 82, 85, 92, 94, 98, 99, 100, 102, 104, 105, 106, 110, 118, 128, 132, 133, 134, 138, 141, 146, 147, 149, 150, 153, 154, 155, 169, 170, 181t, 182, 184, 192, 194, 198, 199, 202, 203

Topfoto: 75, 78

Wellcome Collection: 190

Wikimedia Commons: 7, 8, 30, 32l, 38, 49b, 53t, 76, 77, 81t, 87t, 88, 91, 93, 95, 96 (x2), 97, 103 (x2), 104b, 107, 111, 113 (x2), 114, 117, 119, 120, 121 (x2), 122, 123, 125, 137 (x2), 143, 144, 144, 145, 148, 156, 163b, 164t, 165b, 167, 181b, 183, 185, 188, 193t, 195, 196r, 200, 204